WILLIAMS-SONOMA KITCHEN LIBRARY

Pasta

General Editor
Chuck Williams

Recipes
Lorenza de' Medici

Photography
Allan Rosenberg

TIME LIFE BOOKS

Time-Life Books
is a division of TIME LIFE INC.,
a wholly owned subsidiary of
THE TIME INC. BOOK COMPANY

President: John M. Fahey

TIME-LIFE BOOKS
President: Mary Davis
Publisher: Robert H. Smith
Vice President and Associate Publisher: Trevor Lunn
Vice President and Associate Publisher: Susan J. Maruyama
Director of Special Markets: Frances C. Mangan
Marketing Director: Regina Hall
Editorial Director: Donia Ann Steele

WILLIAMS-SONOMA
Founder/Vice-Chairman: Chuck Williams

WELDON OWEN INC.
President: John Owen
Publisher: Wendely Harvey
Senior Editor: Laurie Wertz
Consulting Editor: Norman Kolpas
Copy Editor: Sharon Silva
Recipe Translation: Jennifer Grillo
Design: John Bull, The Book Design Company
Production: Stephanie Sherman, Mick Bagnato
Food Photographer: Allan Rosenberg
Associate Food Photographer: Allen V. Lott
Primary Food & Prop Stylist: Sandra Griswold
Food Stylist: Heidi Gintner
Prop Assistant: Karen Nicks
Glossary Illustrations: Alice Harth

The Williams-Sonoma Kitchen Library
conceived and produced by Weldon Owen Inc.
814 Montgomery St., San Francisco, CA 94133

In collaboration with Williams-Sonoma
100 North Point, San Francisco, CA 94133

Production by Mandarin Offset, Hong Kong.
Printed in Hong Kong

A Weldon Owen Production

Library of Congress
Cataloging-in-Publication Data:

De' Medici Stucchi, Lorenza, 1926-
Pasta / general editor, Chuck Williams ; recipes, Lorenza de' Medici ; photographs, Allan Rosenberg.
p. cm. — (The Williams-Sonoma kitchen library)
Includes index.
ISBN 0-7835-0212-5
—ISBN 0-7835-0213-3
1. Cookery (Pasta) I. Williams, Chuck. II. Title. III. Series.
TX809.M17D43 1992
641.8'22—dc20 92-10314
CIP

Contents

Introduction

"Pass the pasta!" Who could have imagined, just a few decades ago, that these words would so frequently be on the lips of food lovers everywhere?

Once, we spoke only of spaghetti and tomato sauce or macaroni and cheese, with the occasional mention of ravioli or lasagna. Now angel hair and fusilli, fettuccine and taglierini are familiar terms. And myriad toppings, from simple glistenings of oil or butter to quickly sautéed vegetables, fresh seafood and rich cheese sauces, make every pasta meal a new adventure.

At last, we know what the Italians knew all along, that pasta is easy to prepare, versatile and exceptionally good for us. By stocking a few basics, you can come home any night and have a delicious, satisfying dinner ready to serve within a half hour. Virtually anything—yesterday's leftover chicken, some fresh vegetables, a chunk of Parmesan—can be turned into a simple, quick pasta topping. And for the diet-conscious, pasta, judiciously topped, is an ideal main course, high in complex carbohydrates and low in fat.

This book celebrates pasta in all its variety. The following pages cover the fundamentals, from equipment to cooking techniques, from choosing dried pasta shapes to making fresh pasta. Then come 45 simple recipes, divided into sections on dried and fresh pasta dishes, along with filled and molded pastas.

Please regard all these recipes as inspirational starting points for your own culinary experiments. Don't even feel that you have to make pasta from scratch if a recipe calls for it. Instead, use one of the excellent commercial varieties of fresh pasta now widely available, or a good-quality dried pasta.

Pasta is undeniably here to stay. And one of the greatest aspects of its enduring appeal is its ease. Relax, and enjoy—just minutes from now—a delicious pasta meal that you've prepared yourself.

Chuck Williams

ACCIUGHE
AGOSTINO RECCA
Bufale

Equipment

All the tools you might need to mix, make, shape, cook, sauce and serve fresh or dried pasta

A pot, a strainer and a serving dish will put a pasta meal on the table. But those who love to cook pasta find that their supply of tools grows with their repertoire of recipes.

Large pots help cook quantities of pasta in the abundant water they require. Models specifically tailored to pasta include strainer inserts that simplify draining.

Making fresh pasta requires only a few additional tools. In fact, if you opt for the traditional Italian method (see pages 10–11), you probably already have everything you need.

All that remains to do is to serve the pasta. Here, too, a few more simple pieces of equipment help you achieve maximum enjoyment.

1. Ring Mold
Circular mold with a center hole, for baking relatively moist pasta mixtures or those that might quickly overbake.

2. Baking Dish
For moist or layered baked pastas intended to be served directly from the dish. Choose heavy, heatproof porcelain, glazed earthenware or glass.

3. Electric Pasta Machine
Mixes and kneads fresh pasta dough, which is then rolled and cut with cylindrical attachments.

4. Cutting Wheels
Plain or fluted stainless-steel wheels for cutting fresh pasta ribbons or filled pasta. Choose a model with a sturdy handle and a sharp blade that rolls easily.

5. Pasta Serving Forks
Wooden tines pick up long, slippery strands.

6. Garlic Press
For mashing fresh garlic cloves. Choose a model—usually cast aluminum—that feels comfortable in the hand and has a sturdy, durable hinge and a plastic cleaning tool.

7. Rectangular Lasagna Pan
Enameled, stainless-steel, earthenware or porcelain pan for baking layered pasta dishes.

8. Manual Pasta Machine
Classic stainless-steel model rolls out and cuts freshly made pasta dough. Available in a range of sizes.

9. Pasta Strainer Basket
Fits inside any pot 8 inches (20 cm) or more in diameter. Fine aluminum mesh lets boiling water circulate freely and drains pasta quickly when basket is lifted out by the handle.

10. Mortar and Pestle
For crushing dried herbs, mashing garlic and grinding sauces by hand. Marble mortar provides stable weight, and its unpolished bowl gives a good grinding surface. Brass, glass and ceramic models are also available.

11. Pasta Pot
Large stainless-steel pot includes strainer insert and vented lid that allows water to return to a boil quickly without boiling over.

12. Dough Scraper
For lifting fresh pasta dough and cleaning work surfaces. Choose a sturdy stainless-steel scraper with metal or wooden handle.

13. Pasta Serving Bowls
Traditional Italian-designed shallow bowls, in heavy earthenware, provide the best shape for mixing, serving and eating pasta with sauces.

14. Slotted Spoon
For lifting and draining cooked filled pasta.

15. Cheese Graters
Rotary or half-cylindrical models quickly shred or grate hard cheeses such as Parmesan.

16. Paring Knife
For cutting fresh pasta into ribbons, for cutting ravioli and for general use.

DRIED PASTA

A gallery of shapes, sizes, colors and flavors to suit every recipe and every taste

Factory-produced dried pasta, made by machine from a flour-and-water dough, has existed for more than a century. In that time, its manufacturers—inspired by centuries of Italian cooks who made their own imaginative pastas by hand—have come up with a cornucopia of different pastas.

By some estimates, there are more than 400 distinct commercial pasta shapes, a matter further confused by the fact that the same shape may go by different names in different parts of Italy, and the same name may well refer to different shapes. Still further, pastas are now made in a variety of flavors and with many different flours.

The photograph and captions here offer some basic guidance to predominant pasta varieties. But the most important thing to remember when it comes to selecting, cooking and serving dried pasta is that they are interchangeable. If you can't find a particular type called for in a recipe, simply use a pasta of similar size or shape.

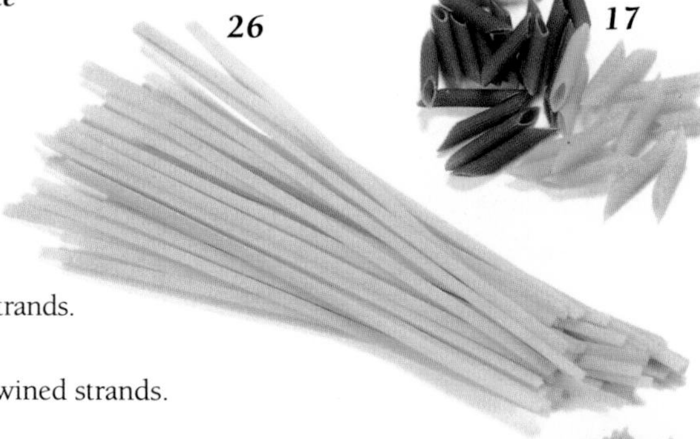

1. *Linguine*
"Small tongues." Long, thin, flat strands.

2. *Taglierini*
Small, narrow ribbons.

3. *Whole-Wheat Fedelini*
Thin, spaghettilike strands.

4. *Rainbow Linguine*
Nests of linguine made from egg, spinach and beet doughs.

5. *Ziti*
Tubes; in short ("tagliati") and long forms.

6. *Fusilli*
Small, corkscrew-shaped tubes. Also known as tortiglioni, spirali or eliche.

7. *Spinach Armoniche*
Spinach dough shaped to resemble small harmonicas.

8. *Conchigliette*
Small shells.

9. *Elbow Macaroni*
Small, short, curved tubes.

10. *Spaghetti*
Classic round strands.

11. *Gemelli*
"Twins." Intertwined strands.

12. *Fusilli*
Long, twisted strands. Also known as spirali or tortiglioni.

13. *Conchiglie*
"Conch shells."

14. *Semi di Melone*
"Melon seeds." Usually served in soups. Similar to the ricelike shapes known as orzo.

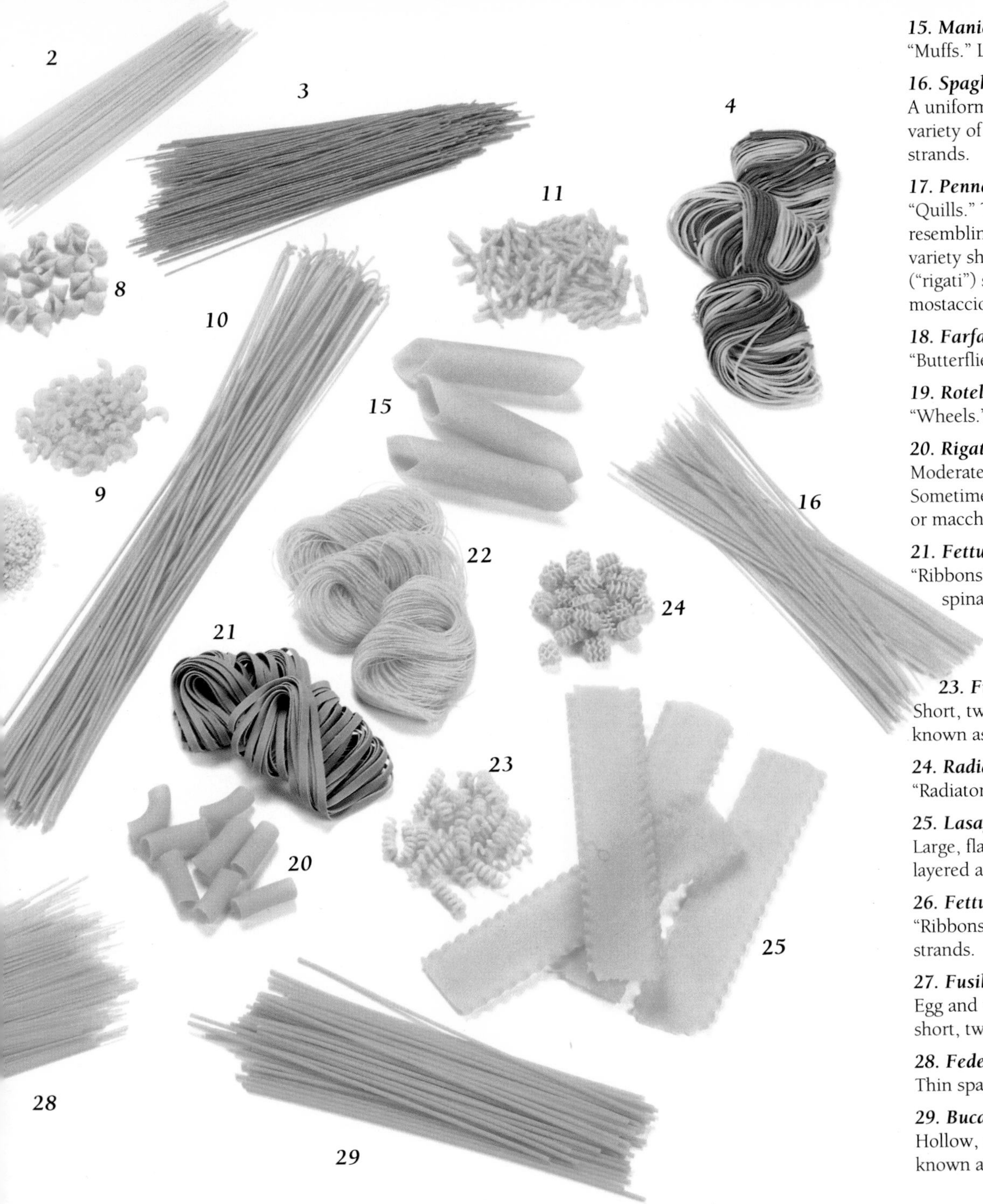

15. Manicotti
"Muffs." Large tubes for stuffing.

16. Spaghetti
A uniform, moderately long variety of the classic round strands.

17. Penne
"Quills." Tubes with angled ends resembling pen nibs. Spinach variety shown has ridged ("rigati") surfaces. Also known as mostaccioli ("little moustaches").

18. Farfalle
"Butterflies." Also called bow ties.

19. Rotelle
"Wheels." Also known as ruote.

20. Rigatoni
Moderately sized ridged tubes. Sometimes called manicotti rigati or maccheroni napoletani.

21. Fettuccine Verde
"Ribbons" made from green spinach dough.

22. Capelli d'angelo
"Angel hair."

23. Fusilli
Short, twisted strands. Also known as eliche or spirali.

24. Radiatori
"Radiators."

25. Lasagne
Large, flat pasta traditionally layered and baked.

26. Fettuccine
"Ribbons." Classic long, flat strands.

27. Fusilli
Egg and whole-wheat versions of short, twisted ribbons.

28. Fedelini
Thin spaghetti.

29. Bucatini
Hollow, spaghettilike rods. Also known as perciatelli.

Fresh Egg Pasta

Pasta Fresca

Cooks today have discovered what Italian home cooks knew all along: that egg-and-flour pasta is incredibly easy to make at home. Whether you do it by hand or use a machine, you can have fresh pasta ready to cook and eat in minutes. Contrary to what some modern aficionados of fresh pasta might think, Italians do not regard it as better than dried pasta; it is simply different.

The proportions given below for fresh pasta ingredients are approximate, and may vary with the actual size of the eggs you use, how you measure the flour, the absorbency of the flour, and how dry or humid the weather is when you make the pasta. In the end, your eyes and your hands are the best judges of how the fresh pasta is proceeding, so pay careful attention to the visual and tactile cues in the recipe.

2⅓ cups (10 oz/300 g) all-purpose (plain) flour, plus ½ cup (2 oz/60 g) for board and extra for sprinkling
3 extra-large eggs

HAND METHOD: Heap the 2⅓ cups (10 oz/300 g) flour on a pastry board. Make a well in the center and break the eggs into it. Using a fork lightly beat the eggs. With a circular movement, gradually incorporate the flour from the walls of the well. Continue until all of it is incorporated. Using the palm and heel of your hand, knead the dough as you would bread dough, pushing it against the board and turning it constantly, until it is smooth, elastic and not too soft, at least 5 minutes.

FOOD PROCESSOR METHOD: Combine the flour and eggs in the work bowl fitted with the metal blade. Pulse briefly a few times to combine the ingredients. Then process using long pulses only until the dough forms a ball around the blade, about 1 minute. Turn the dough out onto a pastry board and knead with the palm of your hand as described above.

ROLLING OUT THE DOUGH: To roll out the pasta, dust a clean board with the ½ cup (2 oz/60 g) flour. Flatten the ball of dough with the palm of your hand and roll it out evenly, always rolling away from you and rotating the disk as it becomes thinner and thinner. It should be about 1/32 inch (1 mm) thick for tagliatelle, lasagne and taglierini, and 1/64 inch (.5 mm) thick for filled pasta.

Lightly sprinkle a dish towel with flour and leave the pasta to dry a while on it, about 10 minutes, or less if the air is very dry. It should be left until it is neither sticky nor dry.

CUTTING THE PASTA: For filled pasta, follow the individual recipe directions for how to fill and cut specific shapes. You will need only 12 oz (360 g) of the pasta dough to make enough filled pasta for 6 people.

For noodles, roll the pasta up into a cylinder, flatten the top lightly with your hand and, using a sharp knife, cut across the roll into strips ⅜ inch (1 cm) wide for tagliatelle or fettuccine, 1¼ inches (3 cm) for pappardelle, a scant ⅛ inch (2 mm) for taglierini and 4 inches (10 cm) for lasagne. Lifting a few strips of pasta at a time, roll them into little nests about 2 inches (5 cm) wide and place them on a lightly floured dish towel. To make lasagne, cut the strips into 4-inch (10-cm) squares. After being cut into squares, lasagne should also be placed on a floured towel.

Pasta can also be rolled out and cut with a hand-cranked machine. First, cut the kneaded dough into 6 equal portions. Then, starting with the rollers set at the widest opening, roll each portion through all the settings, keeping portions you are not working with covered to prevent them from drying out. Fold the flattened dough into thirds and dust with flour before putting it through each narrower setting. Finally, adjust the machine to the setting for cutting into desired width and pass the rolled-out dough through the cutters.

Makes about 1 lb (520 g) fresh egg pasta; serves 6

Fresh Pasta By Hand

1. Mixing the dough.
On work surface, heap flour and make a well in its center. Break eggs into well. With a fork lightly beat eggs, then, in a circular motion, gradually incorporate flour from sides of well until ingredients are combined.

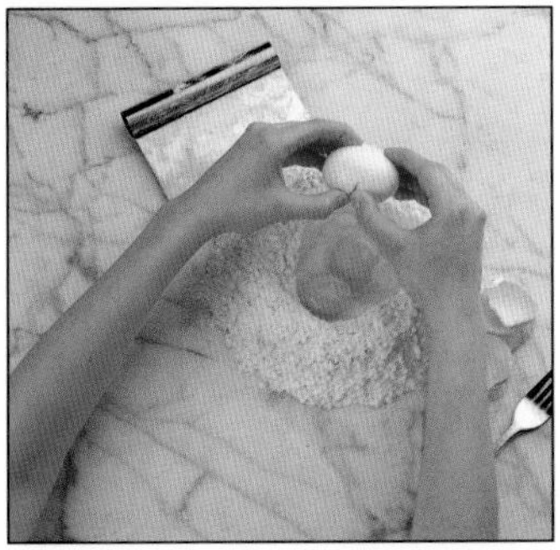

2. Kneading the dough.
With the palm and heel of your hand, and using a dough scraper if necessary to assist you, knead the dough—pushing it down and away and turning it repeatedly—until it is smooth and elastic, at least 5 minutes. If dough sticks or seems a little soft, sprinkle it with flour. Gather dough into a ball.

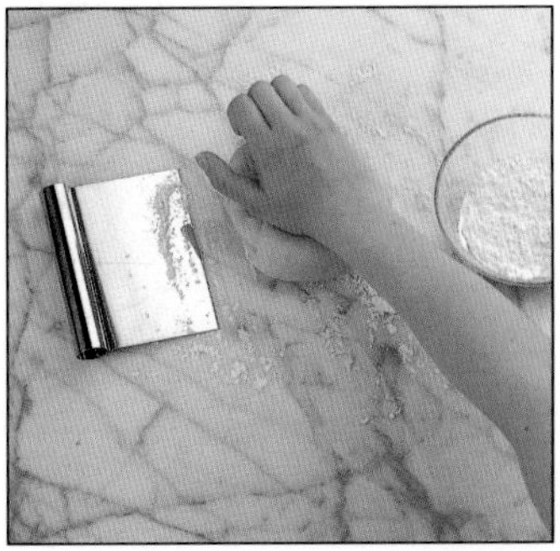

3. Rolling out the dough.
On a clean work surface dusted with flour, flatten dough with your hand. With a flour-dusted rolling pin, roll out dough to desired thickness, 1/32 inch (1 mm) for ribbons such as fettuccine or tagliatelle and 1/64 inch (.5 mm) for filled pastas.

4. Cutting the pasta.
Loosely roll up pasta around rolling pin and unroll onto a flour-dusted kitchen towel, leaving it until dry to the touch but still flexible, about 10 minutes, or less if the air is very dry. On the work surface, roll pasta up into a cylinder. With a small, sharp knife, cut crosswise into ribbons of desired width.

Fresh Pasta By Machine

1. Mixing the dough.
Put the flour in a food processor fitted with the metal blade. Break in eggs.

2. Kneading the dough.
Pulse the machine a few times to combine ingredients. Then process using long pulses until dough forms a ball. Remove ball from processor to a work surface lightly sprinkled with flour and knead by hand as shown in step 2, opposite.

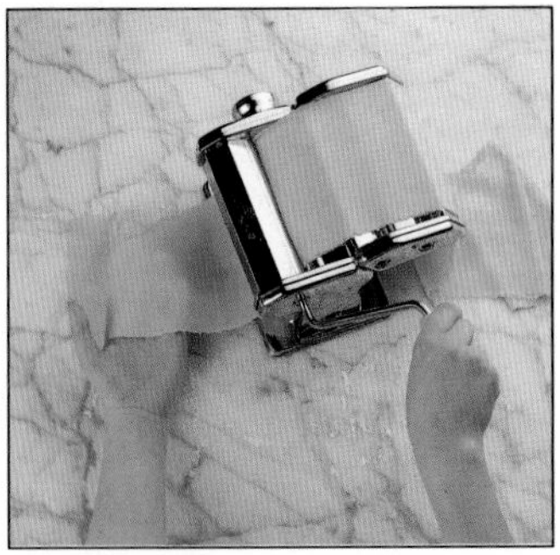

3. Rolling out the dough.
Adjust the rollers of a hand-cranked pasta machine to the widest setting. Cut dough into 6 equal portions. Lightly dust a portion and crank through rollers. Reset rollers one width narrower; lightly dust sheet of dough with flour, fold into thirds and roll again. Repeat process until dough reaches desired thinness.

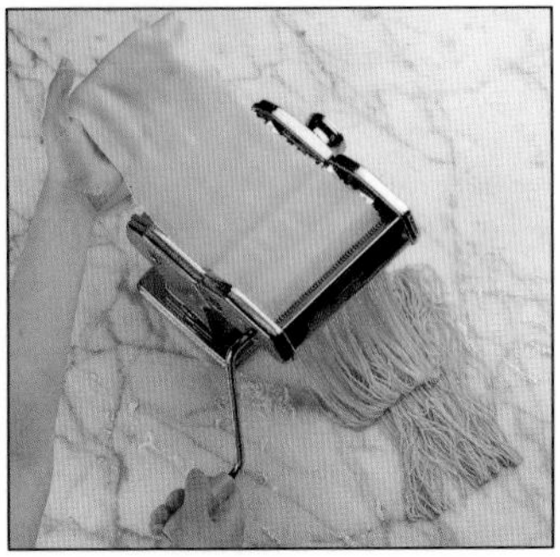

4. Cutting the pasta.
Secure desired cutting attachment to machine. Cut pasta sheet into easily manageable lengths and crank each length through cutter to make pasta strands, in this case, narrow ribbons of taglierini.

Filled Pasta

Basic methods for securely sealing fresh pasta around a savory stuffing

There are many ways to fill and form fresh pasta. Common to all of them, however, is the need to seal the filling securely within its pasta packet so that it won't fall out during cooking or serving.

The demonstrations here illustrate two basic approaches. In the first, a sheet of fresh pasta is dotted at regular intervals with a filling before being lightly moistened, topped with another sheet, and cut into individual squares, as for ravioli or tortelloni.

Alternatively, individual pieces of dough may be cut out and filled, as shown here for cappelletti. The edges of each circle are brushed with water and securely pinched before it is gently twisted into its distinctive hatlike shape.

Sealing Between Two Sheets of Pasta

1. Spooning on the filling. Roll out fresh pasta and, on a flour-dusted work surface, cut it into long strips about 3 inches (7.5 cm) wide—in this case, using a fluted wheel. Place spoonfuls of filling at regular intervals along the strip's center.

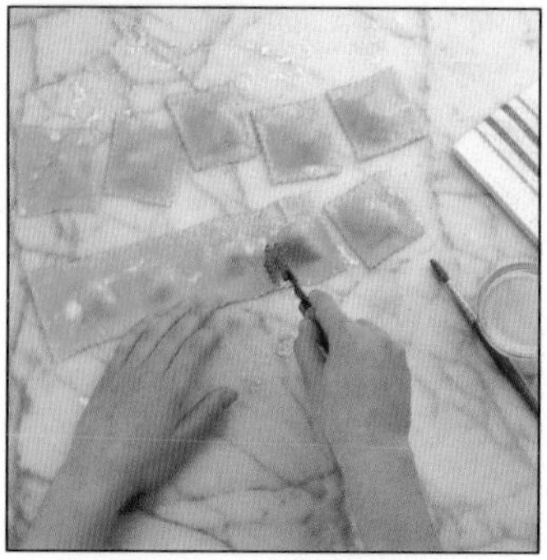

2. Sealing and cutting. With a small brush dipped in water, moisten the pasta along its edges and between each mound of filling. Place another strip on top and press around each mound of filling to seal. With a cutting wheel, cut between the mounds to make individual filled pasta shapes.

Sealing Individual Pasta Packets

1. Cutting and filling. Roll out fresh pasta and, on a flour-dusted work surface, cut into rounds with a circular cutter about 2 inches (5 cm) in diameter. Place a spoonful of filling on each round. Brush the edges of the round with water, fold in half and pinch to seal.

2. Shaping. First fold the sealed edge up to form a cuff. Brush the two corners of the half circle with water. Then, holding the straight edge of the half circle against the tip of your index finger, gently wrap the pasta around the finger and pinch the ends together.

Cooking & Serving Pasta

Simple steps to bring pasta to the table at its peak of flavor and texture

To cook pasta perfectly *al dente*—tender but still chewy—begin with enough boiling salted water to let the pasta circulate freely. For the 1 lb (500 g) of fresh pasta you'll generally need to serve 6 people, 5 qt (5 l) of water are sufficient; use 5 or 6 qt (5 or 6 l) water for the 1 or 1¼ lb (500 or 600 g) of dried pasta needed to serve 6. Cooking time varies with the pasta's shape, size and dryness. Fresh pasta generally takes 1–3 minutes. Dried is ready in 3–15 minutes; check suggested times on the packaging. To test for doneness, remove a piece, let it cool briefly, then taste. Unless otherwise specified, pasta should always be served in a hot dish.

1. Cooking and draining. Bring a generous quantity of water to a boil in a large pot—here, a pasta pot with strainer insert—adding, if you like, about 1½ tablespoons salt. When a full, rolling boil is reached, scatter in the pasta; if the boil subsides, cover the pot briefly to help raise the heat. Cook until the pasta is *al dente*—tender but still chewy. Drain by lifting out the strainer basket or pouring into a colander.

2. Tossing with the sauce. If a recipe calls for tossing pasta in a pan with its sauce, empty the drained pasta into the pan. You might want to reserve 2–3 tablespoons of cooking water to add with it to help the pasta mix more easily. Stir gently but thoroughly to combine the pasta and sauce.

Storing Pasta

Freshly made and cut pasta (pages 10–11) may be left at room temperature until completely dry, and will then keep for up to a week at cool room temperature. The dry pasta may also be wrapped airtight and refrigerated for up to 1 week or frozen for up to 3 months.

Dried manufactured pasta, being virtually free of moisture, keeps well for up to 1 year in an airtight container at room temperature.

Filled pasta may be stored in the refrigerator in an airtight container for 1 or 2 days or up to 1 week, depending upon the filling.

Once cooked, any pasta will keep in the refrigerator for up to 12 hours, after which time its flavor will begin to sour.

Radiatori with Avocado

RADIATORI ALL'AVOCADO

1¼ lb (600 g) radiatori
1 avocado
juice of ½ lemon
pinch of ground dried chili
salt
6 tablespoons (3 fl oz/90 ml) extra-virgin olive oil
2 ripe tomatoes, peeled and diced
1 tablespoon finely chopped fresh flat-leaf (Italian) parsley

Although this is a warm dish, it is also excellent served cold. To do so, toss the pasta with the oil immediately after draining, and then let it cool completely. It may even be refrigerated, but must be brought to room temperature before continuing. Just before serving, gently toss the pasta with the avocado and then sprinkle with tomato and parsley.

In a large pot bring 6 qt (6 l) salted water to a boil. Add the radiatori and cook until *al dente.*

Meanwhile, cut the avocado in half. Remove the pit, then peel the halves and cut them lengthwise into thin slices. Place the slices in a bowl and sprinkle them with lemon juice, chili and salt to taste. Add the olive oil and stir gently.

Drain the pasta and transfer it to a platter. Pour the avocado mixture over the pasta, then toss together gently. Sprinkle the tomatoes and parsley over the top. Serve at once.

Serves 6

Fettuccine with Roasted Garlic and Chili

FETTUCCINE CON CREMA DI AGLIO E PEPERONCINO

6 whole heads garlic
1¼ lb (600 g) fettuccine
6 tablespoons (3 fl oz/90 ml) extra-virgin olive oil
salt
pinch of ground dried chili

Whole roasted garlic heads have such a wonderful fragrance and flavor that you might want to bake a few extra, for guests to squeeze onto crusty chunks of bread. You can also make a similar onion sauce: roast 3 small brown-skinned onions, using the same method as for the garlic heads, peel them and purée with the oil in a food processor. Both versions of the California cuisine–inspired sauce are also excellent at room temperature.

Preheat an oven to 350°F (180°C). Wrap each head of garlic separately in aluminum foil. Place the parcels on a rack in the center of the oven and bake for 45 minutes. Remove the garlic heads from the oven and set aside to cool slightly so that they can be handled.

In a large pot bring 6 qt (6 l) salted water to a boil. Add the fettuccine to the boiling water and cook until *al dente.*

Meanwhile, unwrap the garlic heads, separate the cloves and squeeze the garlic cloves from their papery sheaths into a hot serving bowl. Add the olive oil and season to taste with salt. Sprinkle with the chili and blend together well with a fork.

Drain the pasta and transfer it to the serving bowl. Toss the pasta with the sauce. Serve immediately.

Serves 6

Rigatoni with White Beans and Tomatoes

RIGATONI AI FAGIOLI

- 1 cup (6 oz/180 g) dried cannellini beans
- 6 tablespoons (3 fl oz/90 ml) extra-virgin olive oil
- 3 cloves garlic, chopped
- 20 fresh sage leaves
- 1¼ lb (600 g) ripe plum (egg) tomatoes, peeled and chopped, or canned plum tomatoes, drained and chopped
- salt and freshly ground pepper
- 1 lb (480 g) rigatoni

Simmered together, tomatoes and cannellini beans, the ubiquitous white beans of Tuscany, develop a satisfying, porridgelike consistency. Canned cannellini may be substituted; drain and rinse them with cold running water. If you can't find cannellini, use Great Northern beans.

Soak the beans in cold water to cover for about 12 hours. Drain the beans and transfer them to a heavy saucepan. Add water to cover by about 1 inch (2.5 cm) and bring to a boil over medium heat. Reduce the heat to low and simmer very gently until the beans are tender and most of the liquid has been absorbed, about 1½ hours.

When the beans have been cooking for about 1 hour, in a large, wide, shallow saucepan heat the olive oil over low heat. Add the garlic and sage leaves and sauté, stirring frequently, until the garlic is translucent, about 2 minutes. Add the tomatoes and season to taste with salt and pepper. Simmer for about 20 minutes. Add the beans, cover the pan with the lid slightly ajar and simmer for 15 minutes.

Meanwhile, in a large pot bring 5 qt (5 l) salted water to a boil. Add the rigatoni to the boiling water and cook until barely *al dente.* Drain the pasta and transfer it to the saucepan containing the beans. Raise the heat to medium and stir well to coat the pasta, about 1 minute. Arrange the pasta on a warm platter and serve at once.

Serves 6

Spaghetti with Summer Garden Purée

SPAGHETTI AL POMODORO IN INSALATA

10 oz (300 g) ripe tomatoes, peeled and halved
salt
1 zucchini (courgette)
1¼ lb (600 g) spaghetti
½ stalk white or green celery, trimmed and cut crosswise into slices ¾ inch (2 cm) thick
handful of fresh flat-leaf (Italian) parsley leaves
½ cup (4 fl oz/120 ml) extra-virgin olive oil
freshly ground pepper

Sun-ripened tomatoes join with celery, zucchini, parsley and olive oil to produce a creamy, garden-fresh sauce that is equally good warm or at room temperature. When tomato season has passed, combine the skins of 3 zucchini with either 2 fennel bulbs, sliced and blanched, or 2 celeriacs (celery roots), peeled, sliced and boiled until just tender, and purée until smooth.

Sprinkle the tomato halves with a little salt. Place them cut side down in a colander for about 1 hour, to drain off excess juice.

Using a vegetable peeler, remove the green skin from the zucchini and set it aside. The zucchini itself can be saved and used in a soup.

In a large pot bring 6 qt (6 l) salted water to a boil. Add the spaghetti and boil until *al dente.*

Meanwhile, in a blender or food processor, combine the tomatoes, celery, zucchini skins, parsley, olive oil and salt and pepper to taste. Process until smooth and creamy.

Drain the pasta and arrange it on a platter. Pour the sauce over the top and toss well. This dish may be served immediately or at room temperature.

Serves 6

Fusilli Salad with Sweet Peppers and Mozzarella

FUSILLI IN INSALATA AI PEPERONI E MOZZARELLA

3 red or yellow sweet peppers (capsicums), or a mixture
1 clove garlic
2 anchovy fillets in olive oil, drained
1 lb (480 g) fusilli
6 tablespoons (3 fl oz/90 ml) extra-virgin olive oil
2 tablespoons well-drained capers in brine
10 oz (300 g) mozzarella cheese, diced
12 fresh basil leaves, torn into small pieces
salt and freshly ground pepper

The array of sweet peppers now widely available to cooks makes this southern Italian pasta salad an especially colorful palette. The ingredients, except for the basil, can be assembled a few hours in advance and refrigerated. Creamy Fontina may be substituted for the mozzarella.

Preheat an oven to 350°F (180°C).

Arrange the peppers on a rack in a baking pan and bake until tender when pierced with a fork, about 20 minutes. Remove the peppers from the oven and wrap them in aluminum foil. Leave them for about 5 minutes. Unwrap the peppers and, with your fingers, peel off the skin. Halve the peppers and remove the ribs and seeds. Cut lengthwise into strips about ⅜ inch (1 cm) wide; set aside.

Place the garlic and anchovies in a small bowl. With a fork mash them together to form a smooth paste; set aside.

In a large pot bring 5 qt (5 l) salted water to a boil. Add the fusilli and cook until *al dente.*

Drain the pasta and arrange it on a serving dish. Pour the olive oil over the pasta, add the anchovy-garlic paste and capers and toss well. Let cool to room temperature.

Add the peppers, mozzarella and basil. Season to taste with salt and pepper; toss well. Serve at room temperature.

Serves 6

RECCA
ACCIUGHE SALATE
Peso netto 600 g

Conchiglie Salad with Tuna and Lettuce

CONCHIGLIE IN INSALATA CON TONNO E LATTUGA

For added color, substitute marbled red radicchio or deep scarlet cabbage leaves for the lettuce in this light Genoese salad. Accompany with lemon wedges.

1 lb (480 g) conchiglie
6 tablespoons (3 fl oz/90 ml) extra-virgin olive oil
10 oz (300 g) Boston (butterhead) lettuce, trimmed and shredded
7 oz (210 g) canned tuna in water or oil, drained and flaked
salt and freshly ground pepper

In a large pot bring 5 qt (5 l) salted water to a boil. Add the conchiglie and cook until *al dente.*

Drain the pasta and place it in a serving bowl. Add the olive oil and toss well. Let the pasta cool for about 5 minutes.

Add the lettuce and tuna to the pasta and season to taste with salt and pepper. Toss well and serve either slightly warm or at room temperature.

Serves 6

Linguine with Potatoes and Rosemary

LINGUINE CON PATATE E ROSMARINO

- 1 lb (480 g) linguine
- 3 boiling potatoes, peeled and cut into julienne strips
- 6 tablespoons (3 fl oz/90 ml) extra-virgin olive oil
- 1 small onion, finely chopped
- 2 tablespoons finely chopped fresh rosemary
- salt and freshly ground pepper

A native of the Mediterranean, rosemary flourishes along much of the Italian seashore. Here, in a Genoese dish, its aromatic leaves are used to flavor a simple sauce of potato strips and fruity olive oil. For a different taste, substitute fresh thyme or oregano for the rosemary, or combine the three herbs.

In a large pot bring 5 qt (5 l) salted water to a boil. Add the pasta and potatoes and cook until the pasta is *al dente.*

Meanwhile, in a small frying pan heat 3 tablespoons of the olive oil over medium heat. Add the onion and rosemary and sauté, stirring constantly, until the onion is lightly golden, about 5 minutes.

Drain the linguine and potato and arrange them on a warm serving platter. Pour the contents of the frying pan and the remaining 3 tablespoons olive oil over the top. Season to taste with salt and pepper. Toss well and serve at once.

Serves 6

Fusilli with Sweet Corn

FUSILLI AL GRANTURCO

3 ears white or yellow corn
1 lb (480 g) fusilli
⅓ cup (3 oz/90 g) unsalted butter, at room temperature
2 tablespoons finely chopped fresh chives
salt and freshly ground pepper

This is an especially good way to show off the fresh, tender corn of summer, but frozen or canned corn kernels can be used when the days turn cold. The butter is a northern Italian touch; if you like, substitute extra-virgin olive oil. Although Italians never prepare corn in this manner, they should. The fresh kernels make a particularly attractive, tasty sauce.

In a large pot bring 5 qt (5 l) salted water to a boil.

Meanwhile, husk the corn and remove the silky threads. Using a sharp knife, cut out any blemishes.

Add the corn to the boiling water. As soon as the water returns to a boil, turn off the heat, cover the pot and let stand for about 5 minutes. With tongs remove the corn from the water and set it aside until it is cool enough to handle. Then, using a sharp knife, cut off the kernels and set them aside in a warm serving bowl.

Bring the water back to a boil. Add the fusilli and cook until *al dente.*

Drain the pasta and transfer it to the bowl with the corn kernels. Add the butter and chives and season to taste with salt and pepper. Toss well and serve at once.

Serves 6

Linguine with Basil Sauce

Linguine in Salsa di Basilico

- 1 cup (1½ oz/45 g) firmly packed fresh basil leaves, well dried after washing
- salt
- 3 tablespoons freshly grated Parmesan cheese
- 2 tablespoons freshly grated Romano cheese
- 3 tablespoons (1 oz/30 g) pine nuts
- 2 cloves garlic
- ½ cup (4 fl oz/120 ml) extra-virgin olive oil
- 1¼ lb (600 g) linguine

Basil, pine nuts, garlic, olive oil, and Romano and Parmesan cheeses are blended together for this rich green sauce. Tossing the sauce with just-cooked pasta instantly releases the complex mosaic of flavors and aromas. You can also use this sauce on room-temperature pasta, taking care to toss the pasta with 2 tablespoons extra-virgin olive oil immediately after cooking, to prevent it from sticking together as it cools.

In a large pot bring 6 qt (6 l) salted water to a boil.

Meanwhile, in a blender or food processor, combine the basil with salt to taste (about ½ teaspoon). Process until chopped, just a few seconds. Add the cheeses, pine nuts, garlic and olive oil. Process until a smooth, creamy sauce forms. Leave the mixture in the blender.

Add the linguine to the boiling water and cook until *al dente.* Add 1 tablespoon of the pasta cooking water to the basil mixture and process briefly, just to blend.

Drain the pasta and arrange it on a warm serving platter. Spoon the sauce over the linguine and toss well. Serve immediately.

Serves 6

Spaghetti with Shrimp Sauce

SPAGHETTI AI GAMBERI

- 3 tablespoons extra-virgin olive oil
- 1 small onion, chopped
- 1 lb (480 g) shrimp (prawns), peeled
- ⅓ cup (3 fl oz/90 ml) dry white wine
- 10 oz (300 g) ripe plum (egg) tomatoes, peeled and chopped, or canned plum tomatoes, drained and chopped
- salt and freshly ground pepper
- 1 lb (480 g) spaghetti
- 1 tablespoon chopped fresh flat-leaf (Italian) parsley

Quickly sautéed tomato and dry white wine intensify the sweet flavor of just-caught shrimp in this elegant Venetian dish. For a special occasion, substitute freshly boiled lobster, shelled and coarsely chopped; reserve the lobster cooking water for boiling the pasta.

In a large pot bring 5 qt (5 l) salted water to a boil.

In a large frying pan, heat the olive oil over low heat. Add the onion and sauté, stirring frequently, until translucent, about 3 minutes. Add the shrimp, raise the heat to medium and cook, stirring constantly, for 2 minutes. Add the wine and continue cooking until it evaporates, about 2 minutes. Add the tomatoes and season to taste with salt and pepper. Cook for 2 more minutes.

Meanwhile, add the spaghetti to the boiling water and cook until barely *al dente.*

Drain the pasta and transfer it to the frying pan containing the tomato sauce. Add the parsley and cook over medium heat, stirring frequently, for 2 minutes.

Arrange the pasta on a warm platter and serve piping hot.

Serves 6

Pinot Grigio
Alto Adige
WHITE WINE · BOTTLED BY

Penne with Asparagus

PENNE CON GLI ASPARAGI

3 lb (1.5 kg) asparagus
1 lb (480 g) penne
6 tablespoons (3 fl oz/90 ml) extra-virgin olive oil
6 anchovy fillets in olive oil, drained
salt and freshly ground pepper

Each spring Italians anxiously await the appearance of the first asparagus in the markets and on the hillsides where the plants grow wild. This easy presentation plays off the distinctive taste of asparagus against the sharp, briny flavor of anchovies. At other times of year, sliced fennel bulbs or artichoke hearts may be substituted for the asparagus.

In a large pot bring 5 qt (5 l) salted water to a boil.

Cut off and discard the tough ends from the asparagus. Cut the tender tops on the diagonal into slices about ¾ inch (2 cm) wide.

Add the pasta and asparagus to the boiling water and cook until the pasta is barely *al dente.*

Meanwhile, in a large frying pan heat the olive oil over low heat. Add the anchovies and, with the back of a wooden spoon, mash them into the oil for about 1 minute. Drain the penne and asparagus and transfer them to the frying pan containing the anchovies. Raise the heat to medium and cook, stirring frequently, for about 2 minutes. Season to taste with salt and pepper.

Arrange the pasta on a warm platter and serve piping hot.

Serves 6

Fusilli with Onion and Bacon

FUSILLI ALLE CIPOLLE E PANCETTA AFFUMICATA

- ⅓ oz (10 g) dried porcini or 6 oz (180 g) fresh cultivated (button) mushrooms
- 6 tablespoons (3 fl oz/90 ml) extra-virgin olive oil
- 10 oz (300 g) onions, thinly sliced
- ½ cup (4 fl oz/120 ml) dry white wine
- salt and freshly ground pepper
- 3 oz (90 g) smoked bacon or smoked pancetta, cut into julienne strips
- 1¼ lb (600 g) fusilli
- ½ cup (2 oz/60 g) freshly grated Parmesan cheese

For this recipe from northeastern Italy, you can omit the porcini and add 1 tablespoon fennel seeds with the wine.

If using porcini, place in a bowl with lukewarm water to cover and soak until softened, about 30 minutes. Drain, squeeze out any excess moisture and chop finely. If using fresh mushrooms, cut off and discard the stems, wipe clean with a towel (do not wash them) and slice.

In a large frying pan, heat 4 tablespoons (2 fl oz/60 ml) of the oil over medium heat. Add the onions and sauté, stirring occasionally, until golden, about 5 minutes. Add the wine and porcini and season with salt and pepper. (If using fresh mushrooms, sauté them with the onions.) Reduce the heat, cover and simmer gently, for about 40 minutes.

In a small frying pan, heat the remaining 2 tablespoons olive oil over medium heat. Add the bacon and sauté, stirring occasionally, for about 5 minutes. Set the pan aside.

In a large pot bring 6 qt (6 l) salted water to a boil. Add the fusilli and cook until barely *al dente.* Drain and transfer to the pan containing the onion. Add the contents of the bacon pan and cook over medium heat, stirring frequently, for 2 minutes. Taste and adjust seasoning, if necessary.

Arrange the pasta on a warm platter and sprinkle with the Parmesan cheese. Serve piping hot.

Serves 6

Spaghetti with Escarole, Pine Nuts and Raisins

SPAGHETTI ALLA SCAROLA

⅓ cup (2 oz/60 g) raisins
6 tablespoons (3 fl oz/90 ml) extra-virgin olive oil
3 cloves garlic, chopped
10 oz (300 g) escarole, shredded
salt and freshly ground pepper
1¼ lb (600 g) spaghetti
6 tablespoons (2 oz/60 g) pine nuts

The Sicilians add raisins and pine nuts to many of their pasta sauces, especially those in which vegetables or fish are the dominant ingredients. This bittersweet combination, which stars pale green escarole, is also good with the addition of 3 anchovy fillets or 6 oz (180 g) crumbled sweet Italian sausage sautéed in the oil with the garlic. If you like, substitute radicchio for the escarole.

In a small bowl soak the raisins in lukewarm water to cover for about 30 minutes. Drain and set aside.

In a large pot bring 6 qt (6 l) salted water to a boil.

While the water is heating, in a large frying pan, heat the olive oil over low heat. Add the garlic and sauté, stirring frequently, until translucent, about 2 minutes. Add the escarole, stir to coat well with the oil and season to taste with salt and pepper. Cover the pan and continue to cook over low heat, stirring occasionally, for 10 minutes.

Meanwhile, add the spaghetti to the boiling water and cook until barely *al dente.*

Drain the pasta and transfer it to the frying pan containing the escarole. Add the raisins and cook over low heat, stirring frequently, for 2 minutes.

Arrange the pasta on a warm platter. Sprinkle with the pine nuts and serve piping hot.

Serves 6

Fusilli with Sausage, Cabbage and Tomatoes

FUSILLI CON SALSICCE E VERZA

6 tablespoons (3 fl oz/90 ml) extra-virgin olive oil
1 tablespoon chopped onion
1¼ lb (600 g) Savoy cabbage or red cabbage, trimmed and cut into julienne strips
10 oz (300 g) ripe plum (egg) tomatoes, peeled and chopped, or canned plum tomatoes, drained and chopped
salt and freshly ground pepper
10 oz (300 g) sweet Italian sausage, skinned and crumbled
1 lb (480 g) fusilli

Strips of lacy Savoy cabbage, chunks of tomato and sweet sausage combine nicely with spiraled pasta in this Lombardian favorite. In place of the sausage, you can use about half that quantity of chopped cooked ham or bacon.

In a large frying pan, heat 3 tablespoons of the olive oil over medium heat. Add the onion and sauté, stirring frequently, until lightly golden, about 5 minutes. Add the cabbage and continue sautéing for 2 minutes. Add the tomatoes and season to taste with salt and pepper. Stir well, cover the pan with the lid slightly ajar, and simmer over low heat, stirring occasionally, until the liquid evaporates, about 40 minutes.

In a small frying pan heat the remaining 3 tablespoons olive oil over medium heat. Add the sausage and cook, stirring occasionally, until lightly browned, about 6 minutes.

Meanwhile, in a large pot bring 5 qt (5 l) salted water to a boil. Add the fusilli and cook until *al dente.*

Drain the pasta and arrange it on a warm platter. Pour the cabbage sauce over the pasta and toss well. Sprinkle with the sausage and serve piping hot.

Serves 6

Gemelli with Four Cheeses

GEMELLI AI QUATTRO FORMAGGI

2 oz (60 g) Fontina, cut into julienne strips
2 oz (60 g) Gorgonzola, crumbled
2 oz (60 g) Swiss cheese, cut into julienne strips
½ cup (4 fl oz/120 ml) heavy (double) cream
1¼ lb (600 g) gemelli
salt and freshly ground pepper
½ cup (2 oz/60 g) freshly grated Parmesan cheese

Parmesan is an essential ingredient for this irresistibly rich pasta dish, but there are many substitutions for the other three cheeses. Try Camembert, Brie or scamorza for the Fontina; Roquefort, Stilton or other blue-veined varieties for the Gorgonzola; and mozzarella, Gruyère or another firm-textured melting cheese for the Swiss.

In a large pot bring 6 qt (6 l) salted water to a boil.

Meanwhile, in a saucepan combine the Fontina, Gorgonzola and Swiss cheeses and the cream. Place over low heat and cook gently until the cheeses have almost completely dissolved, about 5 minutes. Stir well and keep warm.

Meanwhile, add the gemelli to the boiling water and cook until *al dente.*

Drain the pasta and arrange it on a warm platter. Spoon the cheese sauce over the pasta, season to taste with salt and pepper and toss well. Sprinkle the Parmesan cheese over the top and serve immediately.

Serves 6

Fettuccine with Fresh Peas and Ham

FETTUCCINE AI PISELLI

- 2 tablespoons unsalted butter
- 1 small onion, finely chopped
- 3 oz (90 g) ham, cut into julienne strips
- 1 cup (8 fl oz/240 ml) heavy (double) cream
- salt
- 2½ cups (10 oz/300 g) shelled peas
- 1 lb (480 g) fettuccine

Springtime peas are best for this classic recipe of Emilia-Romagna, but you can also use frozen peas, adding them to the boiling pasta water first and waiting for the water to return to the boil before adding the pasta.

In a large pot bring 5 qt (5 l) salted water to a boil.

In a frying pan melt the butter over low heat. Add the onion and sauté, stirring frequently, until translucent, about 3 minutes. Add the ham and cream. Simmer, stirring frequently, for another 5 minutes. Season to taste with salt and keep warm.

Add the peas and pasta to the boiling water and cook until the pasta is *al dente.*

Drain the pasta and peas and arrange them on a warm platter. Pour the cream mixture over the top and toss well. Serve at once.

Serves 6

Spaghetti Salad with Tomatoes and Arugula

SPAGHETTI IN INSALATA AL POMODORO E RUCOLA

10 oz (300 g) ripe tomatoes, peeled
1¼ lb (600 g) spaghetti
2 oz (60 g) arugula, trimmed
salt and freshly ground pepper
½ cup (4 fl oz/120 ml) extra-virgin olive oil

This puréed sauce resembles pesto, but the flavor—a blend of sweet ripe tomatoes and peppery arugula—is quite different. If you cannot find arugula, feel free to substitute 1 oz (30 g) fresh basil leaves or flat-leaf (Italian) parsley. The finished dish may be refrigerated for up to 6 hours, although it should be brought to room temperature before serving.

Cut the tomatoes in half and gently squeeze out the excess juice.

In a large pot bring 6 qt (6 l) salted water to a boil. Add the pasta and cook until *al dente.*

Meanwhile, in a blender or a food processor, combine the arugula and tomatoes. Season with a little salt and pepper. With the motor running, add the oil in a slow, thin, steady stream, as for mayonnaise. The mixture should be smooth and creamy.

Drain the pasta and transfer it to a serving bowl. Pour half of the tomato sauce over the top and toss well. Spoon the remaining sauce over the top and let cool to room temperature before serving.

Serves 6

Spaghetti with Egg and Bacon

SPAGHETTI ALLA CARBONARA

3 egg yolks
6 tablespoons (1½ oz/45 g) freshly grated Parmesan cheese
salt and freshly ground pepper
6 tablespoons (3 fl oz/90 ml) extra-virgin olive oil
3 oz (90 g) thinly sliced pancetta or bacon, cut into julienne strips
1¼ lb (600 g) spaghetti

The heat of just-drained pasta cooks the egg yolks in this simple sauce that is a favorite of Romans. Many theories surround the origin of this recipe. Some say it was a popular dish of coal miners (carbonari); *others claim it was long ago enjoyed by charcoal makers.*

In a bowl beat the egg yolks with the Parmesan cheese. Season to taste with salt and pepper.

In a large pot bring 6 qt (6 l) salted water to a boil.

In a large frying pan, heat the olive oil and pancetta or bacon together over medium heat. Sauté until crisp and golden, about 5 minutes.

Meanwhile, add the spaghetti to the boiling water and cook until barely *al dente.*

Drain the pasta and transfer it to the frying pan containing the pancetta. Stir over low heat for 2 minutes.

Arrange the pasta on a warm platter. Pour the beaten egg yolks over the top and immediately toss well to coat the spaghetti. Serve piping hot.

Serves 6

Farfalle with Walnuts and Lemon Zest

FARFALLE ALLE NOCI

1¼ lb (600 g) farfalle
⅓ cup (3 oz/90 g) unsalted butter
⅔ cup (2 oz/60 g) walnuts, very finely chopped
1 tablespoon grated lemon zest
2 tablespoons Cognac
salt and freshly ground pepper

In Italy, lemons from sun-baked Sicily are paired with Cognac from neighboring France to produce this international sauce. Almonds, hazelnuts (filberts) or pine nuts can stand in for the walnuts.

In a large pot bring 6 qt (6 l) salted water to a boil. Add the farfalle and cook until *al dente.*

Meanwhile, in the top pan of a double boiler placed over simmering water (or in a saucepan set in a larger pan halfway filled with barely simmering water), melt the butter. Stir in the walnuts, lemon zest and Cognac and keep warm over low heat.

Drain the pasta and arrange it on a warm platter. Add the walnut-butter mixture and sprinkle to taste with salt and pepper. Toss well and serve piping hot.

Serves 6

Linguine with Sole, Tomatoes and Bacon

LINGUINE ALLE SOGLIOLE

1 lb (480 g) sole fillets
3 tablespoons extra-virgin olive oil
2 oz (60 g) bacon, cut into julienne strips
10 oz (300 g) ripe plum (egg) tomatoes, peeled and chopped, or canned plum tomatoes, drained and chopped
salt and freshly ground pepper
1 lb (480 g) linguine

Strips of delicate white fish and chunks of tomato are tossed with linguine ("little tongues") in this easily prepared dish. Fresh cod fillets or whole peeled shrimp (prawns) may be used instead of the sole.

In a large pot bring 5 qt (5 l) salted water to a boil.

Cut the sole fillets into pieces 2 inches (5 cm) long and ½ inch (12 mm) wide; set aside.

In a large frying pan, heat the olive oil over medium heat. Add the bacon and fry, stirring occasionally, until crisp, about 5 minutes. Add the fish to the frying pan and fry for about 2 minutes. Add the tomatoes and cook over medium heat, stirring occasionally, for 5 minutes. Season to taste with salt and pepper.

Meanwhile, add the linguine to the boiling water and cook until barely *al dente*.

Drain the pasta and transfer it to the frying pan containing the tomato sauce. Cook over medium heat, stirring gently, for 2 minutes.

Arrange the pasta on a warm platter and serve at once.

Serves 6

Marchese Lodovico A.
KOBRAND CORPORATION, N.Y., N.Y.

Baked Rigatoni with Ham and Mushrooms

RIGATONI CON PROSCIUTTO E FUNGHI SECCHI

- ⅓ oz (10 g) dried porcini or 6 oz (180 g) fresh cultivated (button) mushrooms
- 2 tablespoons unsalted butter, if using fresh mushrooms, plus 6 tablespoons (3 oz/90 g)
- 12 oz (360 g) rigatoni
- ⅓ cup (1½ oz/50 g) all-purpose (plain) flour
- 2½ cups (20 fl oz/625 ml) milk
- pinch of freshly grated nutmeg
- salt and freshly ground pepper
- 4 oz (120 g) Fontina or Swiss cheese, cut into julienne strips
- 6 oz (180 g) ham, roughly chopped

If using porcini, place in a bowl with lukewarm water and soak until softened, about 30 minutes. Drain, squeeze out excess water and chop finely; set aside. If using fresh mushrooms, cut off and discard the stems, wipe clean with a towel and thinly slice. In a frying pan over medium heat, melt 2 tablespoons butter. Add the sliced fresh mushrooms and sauté for 2 minutes. Remove from the heat.

In a large pot bring 5 qt (5 l) salted water to a boil. Add the rigatoni and cook for about 6 minutes; they should be very *al dente.* Drain the pasta and transfer it to a bowl. Add 2½ tablespoons of the butter and toss well.

Preheat an oven to 350°F (180°C). In a saucepan melt 2½ tablespoons of the butter over medium heat. Add the flour and stir until smooth, about 2 minutes. Stirring constantly, gradually add the milk. Continue to stir until it thickens and is smooth and creamy, about 10 minutes. Remove from the heat, add the porcini or fresh mushrooms, sprinkle with the nutmeg and stir well. Season to taste with salt and pepper.

Grease an 8-by-12-inch (20-by-30-cm) ovenproof dish with the remaining butter. Arrange one third of the rigatoni in the dish. Sprinkle one third of the cheese and ham over the top and spoon on one third of the sauce. Repeat the layers in the same order two more times, ending with sauce.

Place in the oven and bake until heated through and bubbly, about 20 minutes. Serve at once.

Serves 6

Fedelini with Bread Crumbs, Garlic and Olive Oil

FEDELINI CON LE BRICIOLE

- 1¼ lb (600 g) fedelini
- ½ cup (4 fl oz/120 ml) extra-virgin olive oil
- 3 cloves garlic, finely chopped
- 6 oz (180 g) fairly stale coarse country bread, crusts discarded and bread crumbled
- salt and freshly ground pepper

Both the Tuscans and Apulians excel at simple pasta sauces that combine bread crumbs, garlic and a fruity olive oil. The Apulians sometimes add anchovies to this old-fashioned sauce as well. If you wish to include some, mash 3 fillets into the oil at the same time you are sautéing the garlic.

In a large pot bring 6 qt (6 l) salted water to a boil. Add the fedelini and cook until *al dente.*

Meanwhile, in a frying pan heat the olive oil over medium heat. Add the garlic and sauté, stirring frequently, until it starts to change color, about 3 minutes. Add the bread crumbs and continue stirring until toasted, about 2 minutes.

Drain the pasta and arrange it on a warm platter. Pour the bread crumb mixture over the top and season to taste with salt and pepper. Toss well and serve piping hot.

Serves 6

Penne with Carrots and Chèvre

PENNE CON CAROTE E FORMAGGIO DI CAPRA

- 6 tablespoons (3 fl oz/90 ml) extra-virgin olive oil
- 10 oz (300 g) carrots, peeled and cut crosswise into slices about 1/16 inch (2 mm) thick
- salt
- 1 lb (480 g) penne
- 6 oz (180 g) chèvre
- 1 tablespoon chopped fresh flat-leaf (Italian) parsley

The sweet flavor of carrots brings out a corresponding sweetness in fresh, creamy goat cheese. While regular pasta may be used, green spinach pasta makes a beautiful backdrop to the other ingredients.

In a large pot bring 5 qt (5 l) salted water to a boil.

While the water is heating, in a large frying pan heat the olive oil over medium heat. Add the carrots and sauté, stirring occasionally, until tender when pierced with a fork, about 10 minutes. Season to taste with salt.

Add the penne to the boiling water and cook until barely *al dente*. Meanwhile, crumble the chèvre onto a plate and set aside.

Drain the pasta and transfer it to the frying pan containing the carrots. Cook over medium heat, stirring frequently, for about 2 minutes.

Arrange the pasta on a warm platter. Sprinkle the crumbled cheese and parsley over the top and serve at once.

Serves 6

EPE

Pappardelle with Chicken Livers, Sage and Bacon

PAPPARDELLE AI FEGATINI DI POLLO

1 lb (520 g) pappardelle *(recipe on page 10)*
¼ cup (2 oz/60 g) unsalted butter
2 oz (60 g) bacon, cut into julienne strips
20 fresh sage leaves
10 oz (300 g) chicken livers, trimmed and cut into slices ¾ inch (2 cm) thick
salt and freshly ground pepper

There is a home-style simplicity to this combination of broad ribbons of fresh pasta and gently sautéed chicken livers. For an equally satisfying dish, use sliced kidneys or strips of chicken breast or veal escalopes for the livers.

Prepare the pappardelle according to the directions for basic egg pasta.

In a large pot bring 5 qt (5 l) salted water to a boil.

In a frying pan melt the butter over medium heat. Add the bacon and sage and fry until they are both crisp, about 5 minutes. Add the chicken livers and fry, stirring frequently, for 3 minutes. Season to taste with salt and pepper.

Meanwhile, add the pappardelle to the boiling water. Cook until they rise to the surface, about 2 minutes.

Drain the pasta and arrange it on a warm platter. Pour the liver mixture over the pasta and toss well. Serve immediately.

Serves 6

Curry-Flavored Fettuccine

FETTUCCINE AL CURRY

2⅓ cups (10 oz/300 g) all-purpose (plain) flour
2 tablespoons curry powder
3 extra-large eggs
2½ cups (10 oz/300 g) shelled peas
½ cup (4 fl oz/120 ml) heavy (double) cream
¼ cup (2 oz/60 g) unsalted butter
salt and freshly ground pepper

Adding flavorings—vegetables, herbs, spices—to regular fresh pasta dough has long been popular in Italy. Here, curry powder adds an exotic touch and a warm golden tint to fresh fettuccine. If you wish, substitute 6 tablespoons (3 fl oz/90 ml) extra-virgin olive oil for the butter; warm the oil briefly in a bowl set inside a pan of barely simmering water before adding it to the pasta.

Place the flour and curry powder together in a food processor or blender and whirl to blend thoroughly. Following the directions for basic egg pasta (recipe on page 10), prepare fettuccine noodles using the curry-flour mixture and the eggs.

In a large pot bring 5 qt (5 l) salted water to a boil. Add the peas and boil for 5 minutes.

Meanwhile, in a saucepan combine the cream and butter. Bring slowly to a boil over low heat and boil, stirring, for 2 minutes.

Add the fettuccine to the boiling water and cook until they rise to the surface, about 2 minutes.

Drain the pasta and peas and arrange them on a warm platter. Pour the cream-butter mixture over the top and season to taste with salt and pepper. Toss gently and serve immediately.

Serves 6

Fresh Basil Pappardelle

PAPPARDELLE AL BASILICO

2⅓ cups (10 oz/300 g) all-purpose (plain) flour
1 cup (1½ oz/45 g) fresh basil leaves, well dried after washing
¼ cup (1 oz/30 g) freshly grated pecorino cheese, such as romano or sardo
3 whole extra-large eggs plus 1 egg yolk
6 tablespoons (3 fl oz/90 ml) extra-virgin olive oil
salt and freshly ground pepper

Mixing fresh basil into pasta dough results in attractively flecked noodles with a subtle herb flavor. This method for making dough may also be used with an equal amount of fresh flat-leaf (Italian) parsley or two-thirds the amount of fresh thyme or rosemary leaves. If pecorino (sheep's milk cheese) is difficult to find, Parmesan may be substituted. For an even more colorful presentation, scatter a few extra herb leaves over the finished dish.

Combine the flour, basil and pecorino cheese in a blender or food processor. Process until the basil is pulverized and thoroughly mixed with the flour and cheese.

If using a blender, turn the mixture out onto a board. If using a food processor, leave it in the work bowl. Make the pappardelle (by hand or in the processor) using the flour-cheese mixture, whole eggs and egg yolk and following the directions for basic egg pasta (recipe on page 10).

In a large pot bring 5 qt (5 l) salted water to a boil. Add the pappardelle and cook until they rise to the surface, about 2 minutes.

Drain the pasta and arrange it on a warm platter. Pour the olive oil over the top and season to taste with salt and pepper. Toss well and serve immediately.

Serves 6

Pappardelle with Stuffed Tomatoes

PAPPARDELLE CON POMODORI RIPIENI

6 ripe tomatoes, halved
8 tablespoons (4 fl oz/120 ml) extra-virgin olive oil
½ cup (2 oz/60 g) freshly grated Parmesan cheese
½ cup (2 oz/60 g) fine dry bread crumbs
2 tablespoons dried oregano
salt and freshly ground pepper
12 oz (360 g) pappardelle *(recipe on page 10)*

This Tuscan dish may be prepared up to 6 hours in advance and refrigerated; increase the baking time to 20 minutes.

Preheat an oven to 350°F (180°C). Gently squeeze each tomato half to release the seeds. In a bowl combine 3 tablespoons of the oil, the Parmesan, bread crumbs and oregano. Season to taste with salt and pepper and stir until well blended. Divide the mixture evenly among the tomato halves, spooning it into the hollows. Arrange, stuffing side up, on a damp baking sheet. Place in the oven and bake, occasionally sprinkling the sheet with a little water to keep it damp, until lightly golden on top, about 40 minutes.

Meanwhile, prepare the pappardelle according to the directions for basic egg pasta. In a large pot, bring 5 qt (5 l) salted water to a boil.

When the tomatoes are cooked, remove them from the oven, but leave the oven temperature set at 350°F (180°C).

Add the pappardelle to the boiling water and cook until they rise to the surface, about 2 minutes. Drain the pasta and place it in a large bowl. Pour 3 tablespoons of the olive oil over the pasta and toss well.

In an 8-by-12-inch (20-by-30-cm) ovenproof dish brushed with the remaining 2 tablespoons oil, arrange the pasta. Cover it with the tomatoes, stuffed side up. Place the dish in the oven and bake for 10 minutes. Serve piping hot.

Serves 6

1990
CHIANTI
DENOMINAZIONE DI ORIGINE CONTROLLATA E GARANTITA
DRY RED WINE
BOTTLED BY MELINI s.c.a.r.l. CALMASINO
AT ITS OWN CELLARS OF GAGGIANO - ITALIA
PRODUCT OF ITALY
Melini

Tagliatelle with Butter and Sage

TAGLIATELLE AL BURRO E SALVIA

1 lb (520 g) fresh tagliatelle *(recipe on page 10)*
½ cup (4 oz/120 g) unsalted butter
20 fresh sage leaves
¾ cup (3 oz/90 g) freshly grated Parmesan cheese
salt

A classic of northern Italy, this sauce of sage and butter complements the delicate flavor of freshly made pasta. Extra-virgin olive oil may be substituted for the butter: gently warm the oil and sage over medium-low heat, just until the leaves begin to darken.

Prepare the tagliatelle according to directions for basic egg pasta.

In a large pot bring 5 qt (5 l) salted water to a boil.

Meanwhile, in a small saucepan melt the butter over medium heat. Add the sage and cook, stirring occasionally, until the butter starts to turn golden and the sage darkens, about 5 minutes.

Add the tagliatelle to the boiling water and cook until they rise to the surface, about 2 minutes.

Drain the pasta and arrange it on a warm platter. Pour the sage-butter mixture over the top. Sprinkle with half of the Parmesan and salt to taste and toss gently. Sprinkle with the remaining cheese and serve at once.

Serves 6

Tagliatelle with Smoked Salmon and Fennel

TAGLIATELLE AL SALMONE AFFUMICATO E FINOCCHIO

1 lb (520 g) tagliatelle *(recipe on page 10)*
1 fennel bulb, trimmed and cut crosswise into paper-thin slices
juice of ½ lemon
freshly ground pepper
6 oz (180 g) smoked salmon, cut into julienne strips
6 tablespoons (3 fl oz/90 ml) extra-virgin olive oil
salt

Strips of silky smoked salmon and crisp, licorice-flavored fennel bulb make this a refreshing, light dinner dish. To serve it cold, toss the pasta with the olive oil immediately after cooking and refrigerate for up to 6 hours. Just before serving, bring the pasta to room temperature and toss it with the other ingredients.

Prepare the tagliatelle according to the directions for basic egg pasta.

In a large pot bring 5 qt (5 l) salted water to a boil.

Meanwhile, place the fennel in a bowl, sprinkle with the lemon juice and season to taste with pepper. Toss well and set aside.

Add the tagliatelle to the boiling water and cook until they rise to the surface, about 2 minutes.

Drain the pasta and arrange it on a warm platter. Scatter the salmon and fennel over the tagliatelle, then sprinkle with the olive oil. Season to taste with salt and pepper and toss gently. Serve immediately.

Serves 6

Baked Pappardelle with Ham and Cheese

PAPPARDELLE GRATINATE

- 1 lb (520 g) pappardelle *(recipe on page 10)*
- 8 tablespoons (4 oz/120 g) unsalted butter, plus 1 tablespoon for baking dish
- ¼ cup (1 oz/30 g) all-purpose (plain) flour
- 1¼ cups (10 fl oz/300 ml) milk
- 8 oz (240 g) ham, cut into julienne strips
- ¾ cup (3 oz/90 g) freshly grated Parmesan cheese
- pinch of freshly grated nutmeg
- salt and freshly ground pepper

If you wish to make this Bolognese dish in advance, substitute a dried pasta such as rigatoni or penne, as reheating would overcook the fresh pappardelle.

Prepare the pappardelle according to the directions for basic egg pasta. In a large pot bring 5 qt (5 l) salted water to a boil. Preheat a broiler (griller).

In a heavy saucepan melt 2 tablespoons of the butter over medium heat. Add the flour and stir with a wooden spoon until well blended, about 2 minutes. Stirring constantly, gradually add the milk. Continue to stir until it thickens and is smooth and creamy, about 5 minutes. Add the ham, about half of the Parmesan and 6 tablespoons (3 oz/90 g) butter. Season with nutmeg and salt and pepper to taste. Continue stirring until the butter melts.

Add the pappardelle to the boiling water and cook until they rise to the surface, about 2 minutes.

Grease an 8-by-12-inch (20-by-30-cm) ovenproof dish with the 1 tablespoon butter. Drain the pasta and transfer it to the prepared dish. Pour the white sauce over the top and toss well. Sprinkle evenly with the remaining Parmesan cheese. Place the dish under the broiler until the top is golden, about 3 minutes. Serve at once.

Serves 6

Tagliatelle with Sweet-and-Sour Vegetable Ragout

TAGLIATELLE CON RAGÙ DI VERDURE IN AGRODOLCE

- 1 lb (520 g) tagliatelle *(recipe on page 10)*
- ¼ cup (1 oz/30 g) raisins
- 1 stalk celery, trimmed
- 3 tablespoons extra-virgin olive oil
- 10 oz (300 g) onions, coarsely chopped
- 10 oz (300 g) Asian (slender) eggplant (aubergine), cut into ⅜-inch (1-cm) dice
- 10 oz (300 g) ripe plum (egg) tomatoes, peeled and cut into ⅜-inch (1-cm) dice, or canned plum tomatoes, drained and diced
- ¼ cup (1 oz/30 g) pine nuts
- 2 tablespoons well-drained capers in brine
- ½ cup (2 oz/60 g) black olives, pitted and coarsely chopped
- salt and freshly ground pepper
- 2 tablespoons sugar
- 2 tablespoons white wine vinegar

Prepare the tagliatelle according to the directions for basic egg pasta. Meanwhile, in a small bowl soak the raisins in lukewarm water for about 30 minutes. Drain and set aside.

In a large pot bring 6 qt (6 l) salted water to a boil. Add the celery stalk and parboil for 2 minutes. Remove with a slotted spoon and save the cooking water in the pot. Chop the celery into a ⅜-inch (1-cm) dice and set aside.

In a large frying pan heat the olive oil over medium heat. Add the onions and sauté until lightly golden, about 3 minutes. Add the eggplant and celery and cook, stirring, for 5 minutes. Add the tomatoes, raisins, pine nuts, capers and olives. Stir well, season to taste with salt and pepper and cook for 5 minutes. Remove from the heat and set aside.

In a small, heavy saucepan, melt the sugar over medium heat, stirring only when the sugar starts melting at the edge of the pan. Continue heating until the sugar is a deep golden color and foams on top, about 3 minutes. Add the vinegar and mix well. Pour over the vegetables.

Return the water to a boil. Place the frying pan containing the vegetables over medium heat and stir well.

Add the tagliatelle to the boiling water and cook until they rise to the surface, about 2 minutes. Drain the pasta and transfer it to the frying pan containing the vegetables. Cook over medium heat, stirring gently, for 1 minute. Arrange the pasta on a warm platter and serve immediately.

Serves 6

Fettuccine with Shrimp and Broccoli

FETTUCCINE AGLI SCAMPI E BROCCOLI

1 lb (520 g) fettuccine *(recipe on page 10)*
6 tablespoons (3 fl oz/90 ml) extra-virgin olive oil
3 cloves garlic, chopped
10 oz (300 g) broccoli florets
18 large shrimp (prawns), peeled
½ cup (4 fl oz/120 ml) dry white wine
salt and freshly ground pepper
1 tablespoon chopped fresh flat-leaf (Italian) parsley

Broccoli's assertive flavor and bright green color marry well with shrimp and freshly made pasta. If fresh artichokes are available, use them—stalks and prickly tops pared, fuzzy chokes removed, and tender hearts thickly sliced vertically—in place of the broccoli.

Prepare the fettuccine according to the directions for basic egg pasta.

In a large frying pan, heat the olive oil over low heat. Add the garlic and sauté, stirring frequently, until translucent, about 2 minutes. Add the broccoli, cover and cook, stirring occasionally, until tender, about 5 minutes.

Raise the heat to medium, add the shrimp and sauté for 2 minutes. Add the wine and season to taste with salt and pepper. Cook for 2 minutes longer. Remove the pan from the heat and set aside.

In a large pot bring 5 qt (5 l) salted water to a boil. Add the fettuccine and cook until they rise to the surface, about 2 minutes.

Drain the pasta and transfer it to the frying pan containing the broccoli. Place the pan over medium heat and add the parsley. Cook, stirring gently, for 2 minutes.

Arrange on a warm platter and serve immediately.

Serves 6

Taglierini with Sautéed Scallops

TAGLIERINI ALLE CAPESANTE

- 1 lb (520 g) taglierini *(recipe on page 10)*
- 12 sea scallops
- 6 tablespoons (3 fl oz/90 ml) extra-virgin olive oil
- 1 clove garlic, chopped
- salt and freshly ground pepper
- 1 tablespoon chopped flat-leaf (Italian) parsley

Quick sautéing with olive oil and garlic transforms sweet, fresh scallops into a delectable topping for pasta. If fresh scallops in their shells are available, they are preferred for this dish. Or try peeled shrimp (prawns) or shelled fresh mussels or clams.

Prepare the taglierini according to the directions for basic egg pasta.

Cut the scallops crosswise into slices ¼ inch (6 mm) thick.

In a large pot bring 5 qt (5 l) salted water to a boil.

Meanwhile, in a large frying pan heat 3 tablespoons of the olive oil over low heat. Add the garlic and sauté, stirring frequently, until translucent, about 2 minutes. Raise the heat to medium, add the sliced scallops and cook, turning once, until tender, about 3 minutes. Season to taste with salt and pepper. When the scallops are almost tender, add the taglierini to the boiling water and cook until they rise to the surface, about 2 minutes.

Drain the pasta and transfer it to the frying pan containing the scallops. Sprinkle with the parsley and cook over medium heat, stirring gently, for 2 minutes.

Arrange the pasta on a warm platter and sprinkle with the remaining 3 tablespoons olive oil. Serve at once.

Serves 6

Tagliatelle with Zucchini

TAGLIATELLE ALLE ZUCCHINE

- 1 lb (520 g) tagliatelle *(recipe on page 10)*
- ½ cup (4 oz/120 g) unsalted butter, softened
- 6 small zucchini (courgettes), cut into ⅜-inch (1-cm) dice
- 1 tablespoon fresh thyme leaves
- salt and freshly ground pepper
- ¾ cup (3 oz/90 g) freshly grated Parmesan cheese

This is a versatile Tuscan sauce. A number of other vegetables—diced eggplant (aubergine), slices of fennel bulb or artichoke heart, small broccoli florets—are good substitutes for the zucchini. If you decide to use broccoli, however, leave out the thyme, as the strong flavor of the vegetable will overpower the herb.

Prepare the tagliatelle according to the directions for basic egg pasta.

In a large pot bring 5 qt (5 l) salted water to a boil.

In a frying pan melt ¼ cup (2 oz/60 g) of the butter over medium heat. Add the zucchini and sauté, stirring occasionally, until tender-crisp, about 5 minutes. Sprinkle with the thyme and season to taste with salt and pepper.

Meanwhile, add the tagliatelle to the boiling water and cook until they rise to the surface, about 2 minutes.

Drain the pasta and arrange it on a warm platter. Pour the zucchini mixture over the pasta, then add the remaining ¼ cup (2 oz/60 g) butter and the Parmesan cheese. Toss well and serve immediately.

Serves 6

Pappardelle with Fresh Marinated Salmon

PAPPARDELLE AL SALMONE

6 oz (180 g) salmon fillet, cut on the diagonal into paper-thin slices
juice of 3 lemons
1 lb (520 g) pappardelle *(recipe on page 10)*
1 tablespoon coriander seed
1 tablespoon chopped fresh flat-leaf (Italian) parsley
6 tablespoons (3 fl oz/90 ml) extra-virgin olive oil
salt and freshly ground pepper
grated zest of 1 lemon

Marinating paper-thin slices of salmon in lemon juice turns them firm and opaque, effectively "cooking" the salmon. Fresh tuna, swordfish or small peeled shrimp (prawns) would be an excellent stand-in.

Arrange the salmon slices in a single layer on a dish. Pour the lemon juice over the top and marinate at room temperature, turning occasionally, for about 1 hour.

Meanwhile, prepare the pappardelle according to the directions for basic egg pasta.

Drain the salmon and arrange it in a shallow soup dish that is large enough to span the rim of the large pot in which you will cook the pasta. Distribute the coriander, parsley and olive oil evenly over the top. Season to taste with salt and pepper. Let stand, turning occasionally, for about 10 minutes, to allow the flavors to blend.

In a large pot bring 5 qt (5 l) salted water to a boil. While the water is heating, place the bowl of salmon on top of the pot and cover the plate with a lid. This will warm the salmon without cooking it. When the water boils, remove the salmon plate, add the pappardelle and cook until they rise to the surface, about 2 minutes. Drain the pasta and arrange it on a warm platter. Add the salmon and toss gently. Sprinkle with the lemon zest and serve at once.

Serves 6

NATURAL SPRING WATER
NON CARBONATED
SODIUM FREE*
NET 8.45 FL. OZ. - 250 ml

Chicken Ravioli with Parmesan

RAVIOLI ALLA PARMIGIANA

8 tablespoons (4 oz/120 g) unsalted butter
1 stalk celery, trimmed and finely chopped
1 carrot, peeled and finely chopped
1 small onion, finely chopped
10 oz (300 g) boneless chicken breast meat, cut into 1-inch (2.5-cm) pieces
¼ cup (2 fl oz/60 ml) dry Marsala wine
2 egg yolks
¾ cup (3 oz/90 g) freshly grated Parmesan cheese
salt and freshly ground pepper
12 oz (360 g) freshly made pasta dough *(recipe on page 10)*
1 tablespoon all-purpose (plain) flour

In a frying pan melt 2 tablespoons of the butter over low heat. Add the celery, carrot and onion. Sauté, stirring frequently, until the onion is translucent, about 3 minutes. Add the chicken, raise the heat slightly and sauté, stirring, until the chicken is golden, about 10 minutes. Pour in the Marsala, lower the heat, cover and cook for 5 minutes.

Remove the pan from the heat, turn out the contents onto a cutting board and chop very finely. Place in a bowl; add the egg yolks and half of the Parmesan. Mix thoroughly and season to taste with salt and pepper. Set aside.

Prepare the pasta dough according to the directions for basic egg pasta. Roll out the dough very thinly. Cut into strips 2⅜ inches (6 cm) wide and 12 inches (30 cm) long. On half of the strips, place small mounds of the chicken mixture at 2⅜-inch (6-cm) intervals. Brush the edges of the strips and in between the mounds with cold water. Cover the filled strips with the remaining strips. To seal, press along the edges and all around the stuffing. Using a pastry wheel with a fluted edge, cut the strips into 2-inch (5-cm) squares. Lightly dust a work surface with the flour and, with the help of a spatula, arrange the ravioli on it.

In a pot bring 5 qt (5 l) salted water to a boil. In a saucepan melt the remaining butter over low heat. Keep warm.

Add the ravioli to the boiling water and cook until they rise to the surface, about 2 minutes. Drain the pasta well and arrange on a warm platter. Sprinkle with the remaining Parmesan and drizzle with the melted butter. Serve hot.

Serves 6

Mezzelune Stuffed with Eggplant

MEZZELUNE CON MELANZANE

- 8 tablespoons (4 fl oz/120 ml) extra-virgin olive oil
- 1 clove garlic, chopped
- 2 Asian (slender) eggplants (aubergines), about 13 oz (390 g) total weight, trimmed and diced
- 1 tablespoon fresh marjoram, mint, thyme or oregano leaves
- 3 tablespoons freshly grated Swiss cheese
- 2 egg yolks
- ½ cup (4 oz/120 g) ricotta
- salt and freshly ground pepper
- 12 oz (360 g) freshly made pasta dough *(recipe on page 10)*
- 1 tablespoon all-purpose (plain) flour

These plump "half moons" may be stuffed with finely chopped broccoli or artichoke hearts instead of eggplant.

In a frying pan heat 3 tablespoons of the olive oil over low heat. Add the garlic and sauté, stirring frequently, until translucent, about 2 minutes. Add the eggplant and sprinkle with the marjoram or other herb. Cover and cook over low heat, stirring occasionally, until tender, about 10 minutes. Remove from the heat, let cool and chop finely.

In a mixing bowl combine the cooled eggplant, Swiss cheese, egg yolks and ricotta. Season to taste with salt and pepper and stir until well mixed.

Prepare the pasta dough according to the directions for basic egg pasta. Roll out the dough into a very thin sheet and, using a round pastry cutter, cut out 2-inch (5-cm) rounds. On the center of each round, place a small spoonful of filling. Moisten the edges of the round lightly with water and fold in half to form a half moon. Pinch to seal. Lightly dust a work surface with the flour and, with the help of a spatula, arrange the mezzelune on it.

In a large pot bring 6 qt (6 l) salted water to a boil. Add the mezzelune to the boiling water and boil for 2 minutes.

Drain well and arrange the pasta on a warm platter. Drizzle the remaining 5 tablespoons (3 fl oz/80 ml) olive oil over the top and serve immediately.

Serves 6

Cannelloni Stuffed with Spinach and Ricotta

CANNELLONI CON SPINACI E RICOTTA

12 oz (360 g) freshly made pasta dough *(recipe on page 10)*
2 lb (900 g) spinach, boiled until tender and drained
1¼ cups (10 oz/300 g) ricotta
2 egg yolks
¾ cup (3 oz/90 g) freshly grated Parmesan cheese
pinch of freshly grated nutmeg
salt and freshly ground pepper
1 tablespoon unsalted butter
1 cup (8 fl oz/240 ml) heavy (double) cream

Prepare the pasta dough according to the directions for basic egg pasta. Roll out the pasta dough and cut into 3-inch (7.5-cm) squares.

In a large pot bring 5 qt (5 l) salted water to a boil.

Meanwhile, squeeze any excess water out of the cooked spinach, then chop finely. In a mixing bowl combine the spinach, ricotta, egg yolks, ¼ cup (1 oz/30 g) of the Parmesan, the nutmeg and salt and pepper to taste. Blend well with a fork.

Have a large bowl filled with cold water ready. A few at a time, add the pasta squares to the boiling water and cook until they rise to the surface, about 2 minutes. Lift out with tongs and drop into the bowl of cold water. Remove from the cold water and spread flat on a dish towel.

Preheat an oven to 350°F (180°C). Grease an 8-by-12-inch (20-by-30-cm) ovenproof dish with the butter. Spread a little of the spinach-ricotta mixture onto one half of each square, leaving the edges of the square uncovered. Beginning at the edge nearest the mixture, roll up the square to form a cylinder. Arrange the cannelloni, seam side down and side-by-side, in a single layer in the prepared dish. Sprinkle with the remaining ½ cup (2 oz/60 g) Parmesan and pour the cream evenly over the top.

Bake the cannelloni in the oven until the top begins to turn golden, about 20 minutes. Serve piping hot.

Serves 6

Broccoli and Tomato Lasagne

LASAGNE CON BROCCOLI E POMODORO

- ⅓ cup (2 oz/60 g) raisins
- 2 lb (900 g) broccoli
- 7 tablespoons (3½ fl oz/110 ml) extra-virgin olive oil, plus extra for baking dish
- 3 cloves garlic, chopped
- 3 anchovy fillets in olive oil, drained
- 1¼ lb (600 g) ripe plum (egg) tomatoes, peeled and chopped, or canned tomatoes, drained and chopped
- pinch of ground dried chili
- salt and freshly ground black pepper
- 12 oz (360 g) lasagne *(recipe on page 10)*
- 6 tablespoons (2 oz/60 g) pine nuts

Soak the raisins in lukewarm water for 30 minutes. Drain; set aside. In a large pot bring 5 qt (5 l) salted water to a boil.

Cut the broccoli florets off the stalks, then peel the stalks and cut them into slices ⅜ inch (1 cm) thick. Add the florets and stalks to the boiling water and boil for 2 minutes. Remove with a slotted spoon. Reserve the cooking water.

In a frying pan heat the oil over low heat. Add the garlic and anchovies and sauté until the garlic is translucent, about 2 minutes. Add the broccoli and cook for about 2 minutes. Add the tomatoes and chili and season to taste with salt and pepper. Simmer until the liquid evaporates, about 30 minutes. While the sauce simmers, prepare the lasagne according to the directions for basic egg pasta.

Return the water to a boil. Have a bowl filled with cold water ready. A few at a time, add the lasagne to the boiling water and cook until they rise to the surface, about 2 minutes. Remove with tongs; drop into the cold water. Remove from the cold water and spread on a dish towel to drain.

Preheat an oven to 350°F (180°C). Brush an 8-by-12-inch (20-by-30-cm) ovenproof dish with olive oil. Arrange a layer of lasagne on the bottom. Spoon a little of the sauce on top and sprinkle with the raisins and pine nuts. Continue making layers, ending with sauce, raisins and pine nuts.

Place in the oven and bake until slightly golden on top, about 20 minutes. Serve straight from the oven.

Serves 6

Cappelletti in Broth

CAPPELLETTI IN BRODO

- ⅓ oz (10 g) dried porcini or 6 oz (180 g) fresh cultivated (button) mushrooms
- 1 tablespoon unsalted butter
- 2 chicken livers
- 2 bay leaves
- ¼ cup (2 fl oz/60 ml) dry Marsala wine
- salt and freshly ground pepper
- 6 oz (180 g) ham
- 2 egg yolks
- ¼ cup (1 oz/30 g) freshly grated Parmesan cheese
- 6 oz (180 g) freshly made pasta dough *(recipe on page 10)*
- 1 tablespoon all-purpose (plain) flour
- 8 cups (64 fl oz/1.5 l) light meat stock

If using porcini, place in a bowl with lukewarm water and soak until softened, about 30 minutes. Drain, squeeze out excess moisture and set aside. If using fresh mushrooms, cut off and discard the stems, wipe clean with a towel (do not wash them) and cut into slices 1/16 inch (2 mm) thick.

In a frying pan melt the butter over medium heat. Add the chicken livers and bay leaves. Sauté, stirring occasionally, for about 5 minutes. Add the porcini and Marsala, stir well and cook over low heat until the wine evaporates. Season to taste with salt and pepper. (If using fresh mushrooms, sauté them with the chicken livers.) Remove the pan from the heat; discard the bay leaves. Turn out the contents of the pan onto a cutting board. Add the ham and finely chop the mixture together. Place in a bowl; add the egg yolks and Parmesan and mix well. Set aside.

Prepare the pasta dough according to the directions for basic egg pasta. Roll out the dough very thinly and, using a pastry cutter, cut it into 2-inch (5-cm) rounds. On the center of each round, place a small mound of filling. Moisten the edges with water and fold in half. Pinch to seal.

Fold the sealed edge up to form a cuff. Holding the straight edge of the half circle against the tip of your index finger, wrap the pasta around your finger. Bring the 2 points together to seal. Lightly dust a work surface with the flour and, as the cappelletti are formed, arrange them on it.

Bring the stock to a boil. Add the cappelletti and cook until they rise to the surface, about 2 minutes. Serve at once.

Serves 6

Tortelloni Stuffed with Herbs and Potato

TORTELLONI ALLE ERBE

- 8 tablespoons (4 fl oz/120 ml) extra-virgin olive oil
- 1 small onion, finely chopped
- 3 potatoes, peeled and cut crosswise into slices ⅛-inch (3-mm) thick
- 1 tablespoon chopped fresh rosemary
- 1 tablespoon chopped fresh oregano
- 1 tablespoon chopped fresh marjoram
- ¾ cup (6 oz/180 g) ricotta
- 2 egg yolks
- salt and freshly ground pepper
- 12 oz (360 g) freshly made pasta dough *(recipe on page 10)*
- 1 tablespoon all-purpose (plain) flour
- 2 tablespoons chopped fresh flat-leaf (Italian) parsley

In a frying pan heat 2 tablespoons of the olive oil. Add the onion and sauté, stirring occasionally, until translucent, about 3 minutes. Add the potatoes, raise the heat to medium and sauté, stirring frequently, until tender, about 15 minutes. Add the rosemary, oregano and marjoram and stir for 1 minute. Remove from the heat and let cool.

In a mixing bowl combine the ricotta and the contents of the frying pan. Using a fork mash the ingredients together well. Add the egg yolks and season to taste with salt and pepper. Stir until smooth. Set aside.

Prepare the pasta dough according to the directions for basic egg pasta. Roll out the pasta very thinly. Cut into strips 3 inches (7.5 cm) wide and 12 inches (30 cm) long. On half of the strips, place small mounds of the herb-potato mixture at 3-inch (7.5-cm) intervals. Brush the edges of the strips and in between the mounds with cold water. Cover the filled strips with the remaining strips. To seal, press along the edges and all around the stuffing. Using a pastry wheel with a fluted edge, cut into 2⅜-inch (6-cm) squares. Lightly dust a work surface with the flour and, with the help of a spatula, arrange the tortelloni on it.

In a large pot bring 5 qt (5 l) salted water to a boil. Add the tortelloni and cook until they rise to the surface, about 2 minutes. Drain well and arrange on a warm platter. Sprinkle with the parsley and the remaining 6 tablespoons (3 fl oz/90 ml) olive oil. Serve at once.

Serves 6

Baked Spaghetti with Eggplant

SPAGHETTI IN FORMA ALLE MELANZANE

- 6 tablespoons (3 fl oz/90 ml) extra-virgin olive oil, plus 5 cups (40 fl oz/1.2 l) for deep-frying
- 3 cloves garlic, chopped
- 1¼ lb (600 g) ripe plum (egg) tomatoes, peeled and chopped, or canned plum tomatoes, drained and chopped
- pinch of ground dried chili
- salt
- 3 Asian (slender) eggplants (aubergines), about 1¼ lb (600 g) total weight, trimmed and cut crosswise into slices about ¼ inch (6 mm) thick
- 1 tablespoon unsalted butter
- ¾ cup (3 oz/90 g) fine dry bread crumbs
- 1 lb (480 g) spaghetti

This typical Neapolitan dish may be assembled and refrigerated for up to 6 hours before baking.

In a saucepan heat the 6 tablespoons (3 fl oz/90 ml) oil over low heat. Add the garlic and sauté, stirring frequently, until translucent, about 2 minutes. Add the tomatoes and chili, stir well and season to taste with salt. Cook over low heat until the liquid evaporates, about 30 minutes.

In a heavy frying pan, heat the oil for deep-frying to 350°F (180°C). Add the eggplant, a few slices at a time, and deep-fry until golden, about 3 minutes. Lift out the eggplant slices and drain on paper towels. Season to taste with salt.

Preheat an oven to 350°F (180°C). Grease a 9-inch (23-cm) springform pan with the butter and then coat the bottom and sides evenly with the bread crumbs. Line the pan bottom and sides with the eggplant slices, overlapping them slightly. Reserve any leftover slices.

In a large pot bring 5 qt (5 l) salted water to a boil. Add the spaghetti and cook until very *al dente,* about 4 minutes.

Drain the spaghetti and transfer it to a bowl. Pour the tomato sauce over the top and add any leftover eggplant slices. Toss well. Pile the spaghetti mixture in the prepared pan and press the top to pack it lightly. Place in the oven and bake until lightly browned on top, about 20 minutes. Invert onto a warm platter and serve at once.

Serves 6

Linguine and Shrimp Tart

CROSTATA DI LINGUINE AGLI SCAMPI

1⅔ cups (7 oz/210 g) all-purpose (plain) flour
⅓ cup (3 oz/90 g) unsalted butter, chilled and cut into small pieces
2 tablespoons water
1 egg yolk
1 cup (8 fl oz/240 ml) heavy (double) cream
6 oz (180 g) shrimp (prawns), peeled
salt and freshly ground pepper
1 tablespoon curry powder
10 oz (300 g) linguine
2 tablespoons freshly grated Swiss cheese

Preheat an oven to 350°F (180°C).

Heap the flour on a board. Make a well in the center and add the butter. Using your fingers or a pastry blender, work the butter into the flour until the mixture resembles coarse cornmeal. In a bowl, beat the water into the egg yolk. Add the egg mixture to the flour mixture and work them together until a soft, smooth dough forms. Pat the dough into a ball, wrap in foil and refrigerate for about 2 hours.

On a lightly floured board, roll out the dough into a round about 11 inches (28 cm) in diameter. Transfer to a 9-inch (23-cm) tart pan with removable bottom. Press the dough onto the bottom and sides. Trim off the top even with the rim. Prick the bottom all over with a fork.

Bake the tart shell in the oven for 30 minutes. If the pastry puffs up during baking, press it down with the palm of your hand. Remove from the oven and let cool on a wire rack. Leave the oven temperature set at 350°F (180°C).

While the crust is baking, in a heavy saucepan bring the cream to a boil over medium heat. Add the shrimp and cook for 2 minutes. Season to taste with salt and pepper and stir in the curry powder. Meanwhile, in a large pot bring 5 qt (5 l) salted water to a boil. Add the linguine and cook until *al dente*. Drain and place in a large bowl. Add the cream-shrimp mixture and the cheese and toss well. Transfer the linguine to the cooled tart shell. Place in the oven until piping hot, about 5 minutes. Serve at once.

Serves 6

Rigatoni and Scallop Ring

SFORMATO DI RIGATONI CON LE CAPESANTE

3 tablespoons extra-virgin olive oil
2 cloves garlic, chopped
2 tablespoons chopped fresh flat-leaf (Italian) parsley
10 oz (300 g) sea scallops, cut in half crosswise
3 cups (3 oz/90 g) spinach leaves
salt and freshly ground pepper
3 tablespoons unsalted butter
¼ cup (1 oz/30 g) all-purpose (plain) flour
1 cup (8 fl oz/240 ml) milk
1 cup (4 oz/120 g) fine dry bread crumbs
1 lb (480 g) rigatoni

Watercress leaves make a crisp centerpiece for this savory ring mold. Shelled mussels can be used in place of scallops.

In a saucepan heat the oil over low heat. Add the garlic and parsley and sauté until translucent, about 2 minutes. Add the scallops, stir well and add the spinach. Season to taste with salt and pepper. Cover and simmer, stirring occasionally, for 5 minutes. Remove from the heat and set aside.

In another saucepan melt 2 tablespoons of the butter over medium heat. Add the flour and cook, stirring constantly, until smooth and well blended, about 2 minutes. Stirring constantly, gradually add the milk. Cook, stirring, until you have a smooth, fairly thick sauce, about 10 minutes. Remove from the heat and season to taste with salt and pepper. Stir in the scallop-spinach mixture. Set aside.

Grease a 9-inch (23-cm) ring mold with the remaining 1 tablespoon butter and then coat the bottom and sides evenly with the bread crumbs.

In a large pot bring 5 qt (5 l) salted water to a boil. Add the rigatoni and boil until very *al dente*. Drain the pasta and transfer it to a bowl. Pour the scallop sauce over the top and toss well. Pile the rigatoni mixture into the mold and press the top to pack it lightly. Place in the oven and bake until golden on top, about 20 minutes. Loosen the edges with a knife and invert onto a warm platter. Serve piping hot.

Serves 6

ALBA 1990
igine Controllata
sco croera
UCT OF ITALY
AZIENDA AGRICOLA
LA MORRA, ITALIA
750 ML.

Fresh Taglierini Ring with Tomato and Mozzarella

SFORMATO DI TAGLIERINI CON POMODORO E MOZZARELLA

1 lb (520 g) taglierini *(recipe on page 10)*
6 tablespoons (3 fl oz/90 ml) extra-virgin olive oil
1 small onion, finely chopped
1 small carrot, peeled and finely chopped
1 stalk celery, about 4 inches (10 cm) long, trimmed and finely chopped
3¾ lb (1.8 kg) ripe plum (egg) tomatoes, peeled and chopped, or canned plum tomatoes, drained and chopped
20 small fresh basil leaves, coarsely torn into pieces
salt and freshly ground pepper
1 tablespoon unsalted butter
¾ cup (3 oz/90 g) fine dry bread crumbs
10 oz (300 g) mozzarella, cut into ⅜-inch (1-cm) dice

This elegant southern Italian dish should be baked as soon as it is assembled, so as not to diminish the delicacy of the fresh pasta.

Prepare the taglierini according to the directions for basic egg pasta. Let them dry completely on a floured board.

In a saucepan heat the olive oil over low heat. Add the onion, carrot and celery and sauté gently, stirring occasionally, until translucent, about 3 minutes. Add the tomatoes and basil and season to taste with salt and pepper. Stir well, cover with the lid slightly ajar and simmer gently until the liquid evaporates, about 50 minutes.

Preheat an oven to 350°F (180°C). In a large pot bring 5 qt (5 l) salted water to a boil. Grease a 9-inch (23-cm) ring mold with the butter and then coat the bottom and sides evenly with the bread crumbs.

Add the taglierini to the boiling water and cook for 1 minute. Drain and place in a large bowl. Reheat the sauce to a boil and pour half of the sauce over the taglierini. Add the diced mozzarella and toss well. Pile the dressed pasta into the prepared mold, pressing the top to pack it lightly. Place in the oven and bake until bubbling on top, about 10 minutes. Loosen the edges with a knife and invert onto a warm platter. Fill the center of the mold with the remaining sauce and serve at once.

Serves 6

D'ALBA 1990
Controllata

Glossary

The following glossary defines terms specifically as they relate to pasta and its preparation. Included are major and unusual ingredients and basic techniques.

Al Dente
Italian term, literally "to the tooth," used to describe ideal degree of doneness for cooked pasta—tender, but still firm to the bite. Cooking time will vary with type of pasta.

Anchovies
Tiny saltwater fish, related to sardines; most often used as canned fillets that have been salted and preserved in oil. Imported anchovy fillets packed in olive oil are the most commonly available; those packed in salt, available canned in some Italian delicatessens, are considered the finest.

Artichoke Hearts
A globe artichoke heart is easily prepared. While preparing, dip artichoke repeatedly in a mixture of water and lemon juice to prevent discoloring. First, snap off the artichoke's stem. Starting at the base, break off the leaves until only a cone of them remains. Cut these off to reveal the prickly choke; with a sharp-edged spoon, scrape it out. Pare off the remaining tough green outer skin.

Arugula
Green vegetable, Mediterranean in origin, with slender, multiple-lobed leaves that have a peppery, slightly bitter flavor. Often used raw in salads; also known as rocket.

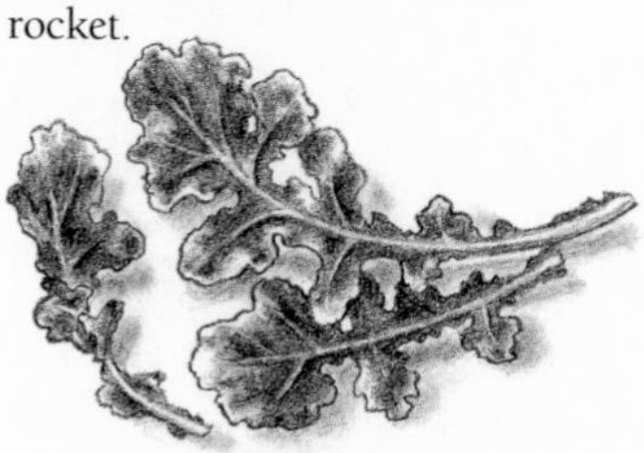

Basil
This sweet, spicy herb is a staple of Italian and French kitchens. A favorite seasoning for tomatoes and, in its fresh form, the main ingredient in pesto sauce.

Boston (Butterhead) Lettuce
Relatively small variety of round lettuce with soft, loosely packed, tender, mildly flavored leaves.

Bread, Coarse Country
For serving with authentic Italian pasta dishes and for making bread crumbs, choose a good-quality, rustic-style loaf made of unbleached wheat flour, with a firm, coarse-textured crumb. Sold in bakeries, such loaves may be referred to by any of several terms, including country style, rustic or peasant.

Brie
Rich, creamy, ripened French cheese, similar to **Camembert,** with a white, powdery exterior and, when ripe, a smooth, evenly soft interior. Usually sold in wedges cut from whole wheels approximately 1½ inches (4 cm) thick and 12 inches (30 cm) in diameter.

Camembert
Rich, creamy, ripened French cheese, similar to **Brie,** with a white, powdery exterior; a smooth, evenly soft interior when ripe; and a slightly bittersweet taste derived from the straw in which it is packed to ripen. Usually sold in whole wheels approximately 1½–2 inches (4–5 cm) thick and 4–6 inches (10–15 cm) in diameter.

Cannellini
Italian variety of small, white, thin-skinned, oval-shaped beans. If using dried beans, soak overnight in cold water (drain before cooking). For canned beans, drain and rinse well before use. Great Northern or navy beans are acceptable substitutes.

Cannelloni
Filled pasta tubes approximately 1 inch (2.5 cm) in diameter and 3 inches (7.5 cm) long.

Capers
Small, pickled buds of a bush common to the Mediterranean, used whole as a flavoring or garnish for a variety of savory dishes. The salty, sharp-tasting brine may also be used as a seasoning.

Cappelletti
Variety of filled egg pasta formed into small, circular hat shapes; similar to **tortellini.**

Celeriac
Large, knobby root of a species of celery plant, with a crisp texture and fine flavor closely resembling the familiar stalks. Choose smaller, younger roots, to be peeled and eaten raw or cooked. Also known as celery root.

Chèvre
French term, widely used outside of France as well, for a number of cheeses made from goat's milk. Most chèvres are fresh and creamy, with a distinctively sharp tang; they are sold shaped into small rounds, about 2 inches (5 cm) in diameter, or logs 1–2 inches (2.5–5 cm) in diameter and 4–6 inches (10–15 cm) long. Some chèvres are coated with mixtures of herbs, with pepper, or with ash, which mildly flavors them.

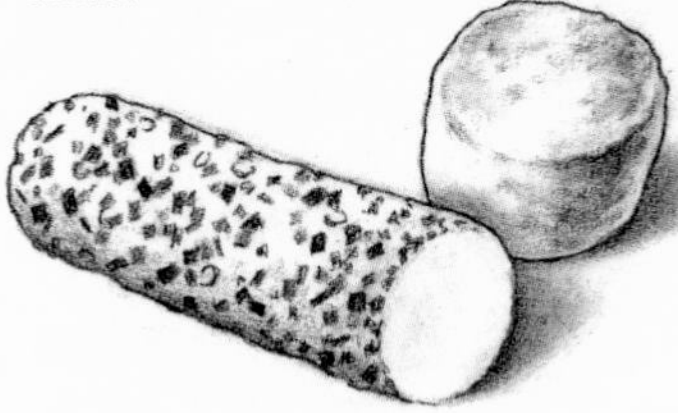

Chili, Ground Dried
Pure seasoning of ground dried chili peppers, ranging in strength from mild to hot. Available in jars in supermarket spice sections, as well as in small cellophane packets in ethnic food sections or Latino or Asian markets.

Chives
Mild, sweet herb with a flavor reminiscent of the onion, to which it is related. Although

available dried in the herb and spice section of a supermarket, fresh chives possess the best flavor.

Cognac
Spirit distilled from wine and, strictly speaking, produced in the Cognac region of France. Other good-quality dry wine–based brandies may be substituted.

Conchiglie
Pasta shapes resembling conch shells.

Coriander Seeds
Small, spicy-sweet seeds of the coriander plant, which is also called cilantro or Chinese parsley. Used whole or ground as a seasoning, particularly in Middle Eastern and Indian cuisines.

Curry Powder
Generic term for blends of spices commonly used to flavor Indian-style dishes. Most curry powders will include **coriander,** cumin, chili powder, fenugreek and turmeric; other additions may include cardamom, cinnamon, cloves, allspice, **fennel** and ginger. Best purchased in small quantities, because flavor diminishes rapidly after opening.

Eggplant, Asian
Variety of eggplant distinguished by its long, slender form. Asian eggplant generally has a finer flesh and fewer seeds than the larger, rounder varieties.

Escarole
Variety of chicory with broad, bright green, refreshingly bitter leaves. Also known as Batavian endive.

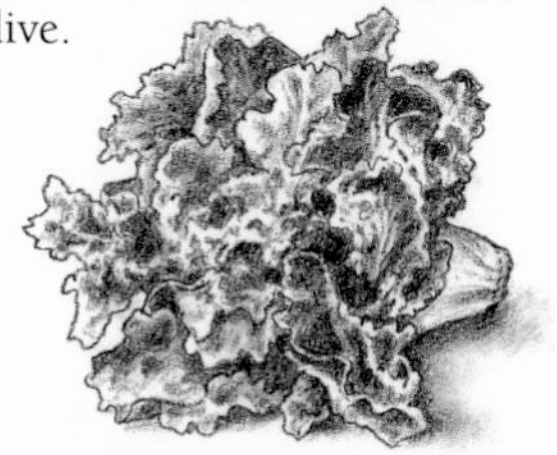

Fagioli
Italian term for any of several different kinds of dried beans.

Farfalle
Dried pasta shapes resembling bow ties or butterflies.

Fedelini
Very fine, spaghettilike strands of dried pasta.

Fennel
Crisp, refreshing, mildly anise–flavored bulb vegetable, also known by its Italian name, *finocchio.* Other, wild varieties are harvested for their fine, feathery leaves, which are used as a fresh or dried herb, and for their small, crescent-shaped, dried seeds, used whole as a spice.

Fettuccine
Long, flat ribbons of fresh or dried pasta, about ¼ inch (6 mm) wide. Also known as **tagliatelle.**

Fontina
Creamy, mild-tasting Italian cheese made from cow's milk.

Fusilli
Thin, spindly dried pasta shapes.

Gemelli
Short, dried pasta shapes composed of two strands—"twins"—twisted around each other.

Gorgonzola
Italian variety of creamy, blue-veined cheese. Other creamy blue cheeses may be substituted.

Hazelnuts
Small, spherical nuts with a slightly sweet flavor good in sweet or savory dishes. Also known as filberts.

Julienne
Refers both to cutting food into long, thin strips and to the strips themselves. To julienne root vegetables, thinly slice lengthwise, then stack several slices at a time and slice again into thin strips; alternatively, use a mandoline or the julienne-cutting disk of a food processor. To julienne meats or cheeses, thinly slice, stack and slice again. To julienne leaves, stack several together, roll up lengthwise into a compact bundle and thinly slice crosswise.

Lasagne
Broad, flat, fresh or dried pasta noodles, commonly layered with cheese, sauces and other filling ingredients, then baked to make the dish known as lasagna.

Linguine
Narrow, thick ribbons of pasta, resembling flattened **spaghetti.**

Marjoram
Pungent, aromatic herb used dried or fresh to season meats (particularly lamb), poultry, seafood, vegetables and eggs.

Marsala
Dry or sweet amber Italian wine from the area of Marsala, in Sicily; widely used to flavor meats, poultry, vegetables and desserts.

Mezzelune
Variety of filled egg pasta formed into half moons.

Mint
Refreshingly sweet herb used fresh to flavor lamb, vegetables and fruits.

Mozzarella
Rindless white, mild-tasting Italian cheese traditionally made from water buffalo's milk and sold fresh. Commercially produced and packaged cow's milk mozzarella is now much more common, although it has less flavor.

Olive Oil
Extra-virgin olive oil, extracted from olives on the first pressing without use of heat or chemicals, is preferred for making pasta sauces. Be sure to choose an oil labeled "extra-virgin." Many brands, varying in color and strength of flavor, are now available; choose one that suits your taste. The higher-priced extra-virgin olive oils usually are of better quality. Store in an airtight container away from heat and light.

Oregano
Aromatic, pungent and spicy Mediterranean herb used fresh or dried as a seasoning for all kinds of savory dishes. Especially popular with tomatoes and other vegetables.

Pancetta
Italian-style bacon cured with spices, salt and pepper. May be sold flat or rolled into a large sausage shape. Available in Italian delicatessens and gourmet markets.

Pappardelle
Flat ribbons of fresh pasta, usually about 1¼ inches (3 cm) wide.

Parmesan
Hard, thick-crusted Italian cheese with a sharp, salty, full flavor resulting from at least two years of aging. Buy in block form, to grate fresh as needed, rather than already grated. The finest variety is designated parmigiano-reggiano.

Parsley, Flat-Leaf
Variety of the popular fresh herb with broad, flat leaves that have a more pronounced flavor than the common crinkly-leafed type. Also called Italian parsley.

Pecorino
Italian sheep's milk cheese, sold either fresh or aged. Two of its most popular aged forms are pecorino romano and pecorino sardo; the latter cheese is tangier than the former.

Chopping Parsley

Wash the parsley under cold running water and thoroughly shake dry. Holding the stems together, gather up the leaves into a tight, compact bunch. With a chef's knife, carefully cut across the bunch to chop the leaves coarsely. Discard the stems.

For more finely chopped parsley, gather the coarsely chopped leaves together. Steadying the top of the knife blade with one hand, chop the parsley, rocking the blade and moving it back and forth in an arc until the desired fineness is reached.

Penne
Thin, narrow, tube-shaped dried pasta with diagonally cut ends; resembles quill pens.

Pine Nuts
Small, ivory-colored seeds extracted from the cones of a species of pine tree, with a rich, slightly resinous flavor. Used whole as an ingredient or garnish, or puréed as a thickener. Also known by the Italian *pinoli.*

Porcini
Widely used Italian term for *Boletus edulis,* a popular wild mushroom with a rich, meaty flavor. Most commonly sold in the dried form, in Italian delicatessens and gourmet shops, to be reconstituted in liquid and added to sauces, soups, stews and stuffings.

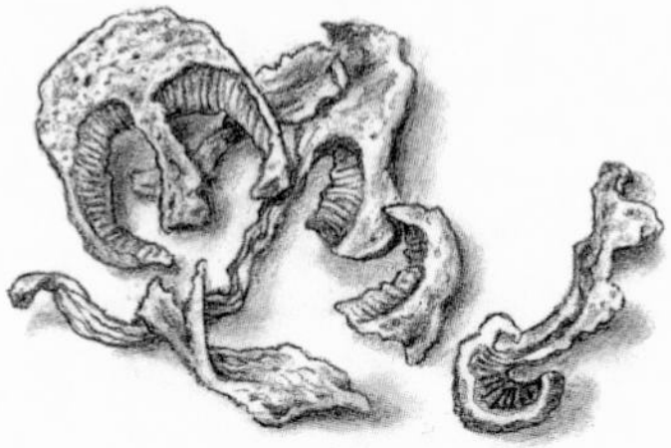

Radiatori
Rectangular, gridlike dried pasta shapes resembling tiny radiators.

Radicchio
Vegetable, related to Belgian endive, whose leaves are reddish purple and have a mildly bitter flavor. Served raw in salads, or cooked, usually by grilling.

Ragout
General term for any thick sauce or stew of meat or vegetables, often served over pasta.

Ravioli
Variety of filled egg pasta, usually formed in small, square shapes.

Ricotta
Very light Italian curd cheese made from twice-cooked milk—traditionally sheep's milk, although cow's milk ricotta is far more common. Ricotta made from part-skimmed milk most closely resembles the Italian product.

Rigatoni
Large dried pasta tubes with grooved surfaces.

Romano
See pecorino.

Rosemary
Mediterranean herb, used either fresh or dried, with a strong aromatic flavor well suited to lamb and veal, as well as poultry, seafood and vegetables.

Sage
Pungent herb, used either fresh or dried, that goes especially well with fresh or cured pork, lamb, veal and chicken.

Sardo
See pecorino.

Sausage, Italian
Fresh Italian sausage is generally made from ground pork, seasoned with salt, pepper and spices. Those made in the style of northern Italy are usually sweet and mild, often flavored with **fennel** seed. Southern-style sausages tend to be hotter, often flavored with flakes of dried chili pepper.

Savoy Cabbage
Firm, round, fine-flavored variety of cabbage with dark green leaves—the outermost of which are curled—marked by a fine lacy pattern of veins.

Scamorza
White, mild Italian cheese made from whole cow's milk, formed into a pear shape, with a smooth, thin rind.

Sea Scallops
Large variety of the bivalve mollusk with rounds of flesh about 1½ inches (4 cm) in diameter. Usually sold already shelled, fresh scallops may sometimes be found still in their shell—complete with their sweet-flavored, orange-pink corals attached.

Spaghetti
Factory-produced thin strands of dried pasta.

Springform Pan
Circular metal baking pan with removable sides secured in place by a bucklelike clamp that, when opened, aids in unmolding. Used as a container for some molded pasta dishes.

Sweet Peppers (Capsicums)
Fresh, sweet-fleshed members of the pepper family; bell peppers, named for their shape, are the most widely available variety. Most common in the unripe green form, although ripened red or yellow varieties are also available. Creamy pale-yellow, orange and purple-black types may also be found. Use sweet peppers raw—stemmed and seeded; or roast them until the skin blackens, then cool, peel, stem and seed.

Tagliatelle
Fresh pasta rolled very thin (about 1/16 inch/1 mm) and cut into ribbons about 3/8 inch (1 cm) wide.

Taglierini
Fresh or dried pasta ribbons about 1/8 inch (3 mm) wide.

Thyme
Fragrant, clean-tasting, small-leaved herb popular fresh or dried as a seasoning for poultry, light meats, seafood and vegetables.

Tortellini
Variety of filled egg pasta formed into small rings.

Tortelloni
Variety of large filled egg pasta; sometimes called **ravioli.**

Zest
Thin, brightly colored, outermost layer of a citrus fruit's peel, containing most of its aromatic essential oils—a lively source of flavor for sauces, marinades and the like. Zest may be removed with a simple tool known as a zester, drawn across the fruit's skin to remove the zest in thin strips; with a fine hand-held grater; or in thin strips with a vegetable peeler or a paring knife held almost parallel to the fruit's skin. Zest removed with the latter two tools may then be thinly sliced or chopped on a cutting board.

Tomatoes
Except in July, August and September, when sun-ripened tomatoes are available, canned Italian tomatoes are far superior to any hothouse variety for making pasta sauces. In either case, use plum tomatoes, sometimes called egg or Roma tomatoes, as they have the best texture for sauces.

To peel fresh tomatoes, follow these simple steps:

Bring a saucepan of water to a boil. With a small, sharp knife, cut out the core from the stem end of the tomato, here a plum (egg) tomato. Then cut a shallow X in the skin at the tomato's base.

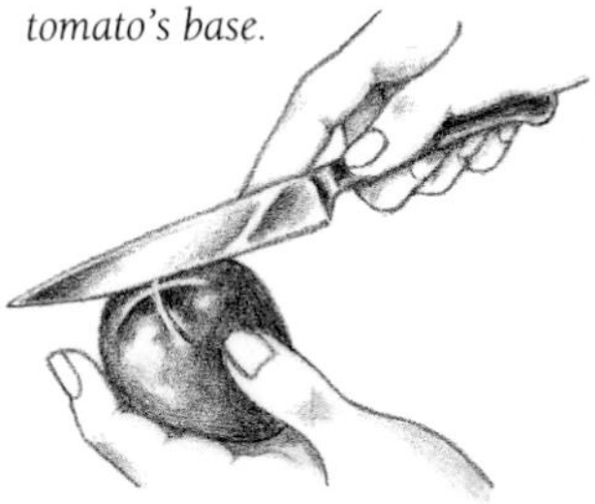

Insert a fork into the tomato and lower it into the boiling water. Leave it submerged for about 20 seconds, then remove it from the boiling water and dip it into a bowl of cold water.

Starting at the X, peel the skin from the tomato, using your fingertips and, if necessary, the knife blade.

Cut the tomato in half and turn each half cut side down. Then cut as directed in the recipe.

If a recipe calls for seeding, cut the tomato—here, a beefsteak tomato—in half crosswise. Holding a half in one hand, squeeze gently but firmly to force out the seed sacks, clearing them away with a fingertip.

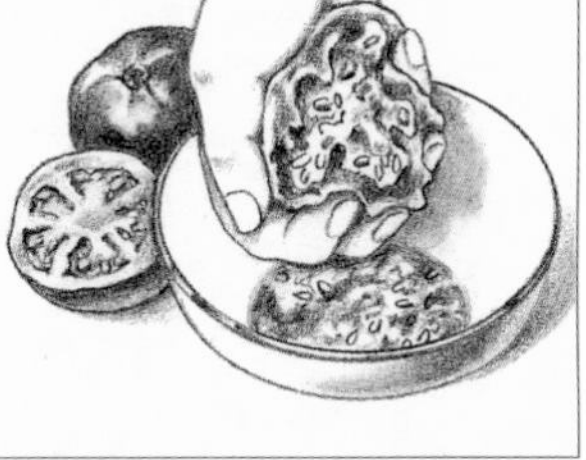

Index

Acknowledgments

The publishers would like to thank the following people and organizations for their generous assistance and support in producing this book: Janique Poncelet, Ruth Jacobson, Jane Fraser, Amy Morton, Ken DellaPenta, Rapid Lasergraphics (San Francisco), Danielle di Salvo, Maria Antonis, Stephen Griswold, John Powell, the buyers for Gardener's Eden, and the buyers and store managers for Williams-Sonoma and Pottery Barn stores.

The following kindly lent props for the photography: Stephanie Greenleigh, Sue Fisher King, Lorraine & Judson Puckett, Gianfranco Salvio, Sue White and Chuck Williams.